HOW I MET
MY OTHER
VOLUME 3
TRUE ENGAGEMENTS,
FOREVER LOVE

HOW I MET
MY OTHER
VOLUME 3
TRUE ENGAGEMENTS,
FOREVER LOVE

Edited by Arielle Haughee

ORANGE
BLOSSOM
PUBLISHING

Maitland, FL

Orange Blossom Publishing
Maitland, Florida
www.orangeblossombooks.com
info@orangeblossombooks.com

Cover Design: Diogo Lando
Interior Formatting: Autumn Skye
Copy Editing: Lauren Stendel

All stories based off true events. Some names have been changed for privacy purposes.

Printed in the U.S.A.

Paperback ISBN: 978-1-949935-32-5
Ebook ISBN: 978-1-949935-33-2

Dedication

To Jon and Mary, for having a beautiful
love story that keeps going

Table of Contents

HOW I MET MY OTHER

Introduction

Rings are circles, signs of the eternal promise two people give to each other. The excitement and anticipation of that one moment, when one person asks another to be together for all their days, can be overwhelming at times. In 2008, I swore to my then boyfriend, Tim, that I would not move to another town with him and leave a job I loved without a ring on my finger.

Christmas came and went, and my finger was still bare. Didn't he want to be with me forever? Tim would graduate law school in May and was due to move shortly thereafter. If I was supposed to move in a few short months, I had to find a new job and a place to live. For me, the clock was running out. In January, we planned a trip outside of Boone, North Carolina for Valentine's Day. This would be a great opportunity—he better take it!

One evening, while chatting with my dad on the phone, he mentioned something that stopped me in my tracks: "So I talked with Tim the other day about marriage."

My heart paused.

"What are you talking about, Dad?"

"He drove into town and we had lunch. He asked me about getting married."

"Dad! You're not supposed to tell me that!"

But secretly I was thrilled. I could finally sleep soundly knowing it was coming. The Valentine's trip now seemed more promising than ever.

Tim and I openly communicate about everything, and I couldn't contain my excitement when I saw him later that day.

"So I had a talk with Dad today."

"Uh huh," he said without looking up from his class notes.

"He told me you drove down to see him and talked about marriage."

"WHAT?" The notes were suddenly forgotten. "He told you about that?"

My smile was a mile wide. "Maybe."

Tim scowled. "Well you don't know when!"

He stomped out of the room.

On the morning of the trip, I kept a close eye on what Tim packed in his suitcase. Maybe I could spot him sneaking a small box in there. No luck. It had to be this trip, right? He wouldn't ask me in May and expect me to move the next day. At least I hoped he wouldn't.

The drive felt interminable, but we finally arrived. Tim's neighbors had graciously lent us their cabin tucked into the Blue Ridge mountains. Bare trees sprinkled with snow scattered over soft, rolling peaks showed through the front window.

A beautiful backdrop for hopefully a beautiful moment.

As Tim unpacked his suitcase, one of his sock rolls landed with a thud in the dresser drawer. Interesting. I kept my smile to myself, not wanting to upset him further. We planned a hike at Grandfather Mountain the next day. Tim mentioned he'd been there as a child and loved it.

I soon learned why. After viewing rescued animals and seeing that bald eagles are as tall as a three-year-old, we headed for the trail, a mysterious winding path through the trees. Full of that excitement and anticipation, I hugged Tim, and felt a square box in his coat pocket. This was truly going to be it!

We stopped at a beautiful, ice-filled stone enclave. No proposal.

Then a small, frozen waterfall with water trickling onto smooth stones. No proposal.

What was he waiting for? Maybe he wouldn't propose on this hike. Maybe he was waiting for me to say or do something, and I would never do it. My mind swirled with doubt.

Then the trees thinned, and an enormous boulder blocked the hiking path. We couldn't go around it, so Tim put out his hand and together we climbed up. I focused on each footstep, not wanting to slip on the wet stone. He helped me up the last bit, still clasping my hand.

I finally looked up and gasped.

Miles and miles of beautiful rolling hills and soft blue mountain tops unfolded in a breathtaking vista. My eyes could barely take in the entirety of the unbelievable view... let alone see what Tim was doing. When I finally looked over to say how amazing this was, he dropped down on one knee, and pulled the square box out of his pocket.

Inside was a promise for the future, a ring.

HOW I MET MY OTHER

The authors in this book share their stories, their moments of forever love, when a promise was made to deeply care for each other forever. Some folks had to wait for just the right moment, like Tim did, others found a second chance at love, while still more were caught by surprise.

I hope you see yourself in some of these tales, and feel the love that flows in perpetual motion, forever flowing back and forth in perfect motion, a circle.

Arielle

Unexpected Beginnings

More Than This

by Stephania Thompson

Skirting the Truth

Stephania

I was freezing.

Should've worn pants, that little internal voice lectured, ticking in staccato to the tap, tap, tap of my heels on the pavement.

"Your skirt's too short," Collin had warned, frowning as I hurried out for work this morning. "You're going to be cold."

Oh, how it burned when he was right!

It might have been June in Baltimore, but the temperature hadn't spiked above sixty for days. If it was this chilly on the city streets, my office was sure to feel like an icebox.

But the too-small, mid-thigh, stretch blue mini wasn't a fashion statement—it was an act of rebellion. Collin hated short, tight clothing, and damn if a little chill would prevent me from pissing him off.

HOW I MET MY OTHER

He and I were on year one-too-many of a toxic relationship. We'd reached that point where every interaction disin-
tegrated into insults, snide comments, and cutting glances.
It was time to jump ship, but my self-esteem had taken a
beating, and I wasn't sure I deserved more than this. And
so, I stayed.

Thankfully, work kept me sane. I'd paid my dues in the
staff accounting pool and had finally landed my dream job
as a financial analyst at a large, well-respected asset management firm. The market was booming, and I was racking
up the hours. One benefit of a miserable home life? You
don't mind the overtime.

I slumped into my cubicle, shivering as I tugged at the
offending skirt, and let out an exhausted sigh.

"What's wrong, muffin?" came the cheery voice of Heidi,
my cubemate. "Trouble in paradise?" Unlike me, the twin-
kling-eyed blonde was never without a smile or an encour-
aging word.

"Always," I muttered, rubbing vigorously at my skin to
generate some warmth. Low wall cubes only allowed for so
much privacy, and with a sea of young accountants packed
onto one floor, drama was forever unfolding.

But that was one of the best parts. Camaraderie.
Friendships formed in the trenches. Did we know far too
much about each other? Probably. But there was comfort in
that. A bond of familiarity forged in the shared drudgery of
account recs, reheated coffee, and late-night revisions. We
were family, albeit a dysfunctional one.

Which is why Heidi wasn't surprised when, five minutes
later, I poked my head above the wall and whispered, "Have
you seen him yet?"

Him, being Terry. Heidi's new boss.

He'd been working a month but remained something of an anomaly. Distant or shy—we couldn't tell—he'd kept to himself, interacting mostly with his direct reports and a handful of managers.

Naturally, the rest of us were curious. And his drop-dead good looks weren't hurting the cause. Solid and ruggedly built, he had golden, sun-warmed skin, silky brown hair, and eyes like twin emeralds. He didn't smile often, but when he did, the room brightened, as if a ray of sunshine had found its way in.

Speculating about Terry had become something of a sport for us girls. A harmless enough pastime. I was with Collin, after all, everyone knew about him. Including Heidi, who'd become a trusted confidant and close friend.

She shook her head. "Haven't seen him," she said, then pulled a face. "Kind of strange, now that you mention it. He's never this late."

My eyes traveled down the row to his desk. *Empty*. Heidi was right, since starting last month he'd routinely beat us in. The telltale sign of his odd little breakfast—a diet Mountain Dew and bag of pretzels—neatly in place long before our coffees were poured. I didn't know much about Terry, but I'd observed enough to learn he was a creature of habit. And dependable to a fault.

"I bet there's a story," I said, almost jokingly, wholly unaware that his story would be a catalyst of change in both our lives.

The Wall of Anonymity

Terry

I was sweating.

Traffic had been at a standstill when I merged onto the beltway this morning. It'd taken an hour to crawl into the city, another twenty minutes to find parking in Federal Hill, and then a fifteen-minute walk to my building from there.

This, after a three-hour ride back to Baltimore from Southern Maryland last night, and less than two hours sleep. I was running on fumes.

And sweating—profusely.

I wiped at my brow, glancing quickly around the crowded conference room. Most of my colleagues had their heads down, or eyes trained at the screen which showed a projection of next quarter's operating budget. No one had noticed when I slipped in five minutes late, and no one seemed to be paying attention now.

Relieved, I sunk deeper in the chair and allowed my mind to wander. It'd been a crazy weekend, celebrating my best friend Jamie's wedding. The party started Friday at the rehearsal, and it hadn't stopped. As a dutiful groomsman, neither had I.

We'd been friends since grade school. But when I left St. Mary's for college and work, Jamie stayed. And he invited half the county to celebrate with him and Megan. Predictably, things got wild at the reception. I grinned to myself, remembering the night's events, then felt the sting of eyes on me.

I looked up to find Steph, a pretty, dark-haired analyst from the reporting team, watching. Heat crept onto my face even as she looked away, grateful, at least, she couldn't read my thoughts.

I tried to keep work separate from my personal life. A challenge, I was finding. This was a tight-knit group, and I liked them. But it was hard, opening up, and I'd wanted to make a good impression.

With a car payment and a hefty new mortgage, I needed this job. And, if the weekend was any indicator, I needed to think about settling down. Quit partying so much and focus on the future. Hopefully find what Jamie and Megan had found in each other.

That's what I really wanted—a relationship. Someone to build a life with. Start a family.

I took another glance around the room. There was certainly no shortage of attractive, intelligent women here. Only, I'd been down that road. Dating a colleague was never a good idea, and not something I planned on repeating.

Yet somehow, a few hours later, I found myself drawn to the tan, shapely legs of one of those very colleagues. A group had returned from lunch and were gathered at Heidi's desk chatting about the weekend.

The legs belonged to Steph. The same Steph who'd caught me daydreaming earlier. Those legs were attached to an equally shapely figure dressed in an eye-popping skirt and fitted jacket. Coupled with glossy hair and a smooth, olive complexion, she looked stunning, if not slightly inappropriate for the office, not that I was complaining. But the way she kept tugging at the fabric made me wonder why she'd chosen to wear it.

Unfortunately, I considered this a moment too long because the conversation stalled and suddenly, all eyes were on me.

"So, what did *you* do this weekend, Terry?"

The question, posed by none other than Heidi, came with a discreet little wink. Confirmation that my appraisal had *not* gone unnoticed.

Wonderful.

Flustered, I blurted out the first thing that came to mind, which, to my horror, sounded something like, "I got tanked at my best friend's wedding."

And my wall of anonymity came tumbling down.

Mostly Professional

Stephania

Heidi leaned against my desk.

"So, I heard Terry was asking about you again," she said in a conspiratorial whisper.

I rolled my eyes. Heidi knew how to stir a pot. And make a girl feel good because I couldn't help a little smile.

"Whatever, Heidi. Isn't he with someone now?" I glanced at my phone with its angry blinking light. "And have you forgotten about Collin?" The message was no doubt from him—I'd been avoiding his calls all day.

"No, but I wish you'd forget about him! He's not worth all the pain, Steph. And he doesn't treat you right. What's it going to take for you to see that?"

Things between him and I had continued to deteriorate, and Heidi was getting a daily earful. What didn't help was her renewed belief in true love. She'd finally untangled her own difficult relationship and was secretly dating Steve, a cute guy from payroll who happened to sit in the same row as us, in the cube opposite Terry. Talk about drama!

I was honestly thrilled for them both. Steve was a lot of fun, and so sweet to her. But I was still bent on salvaging things with Collin. We'd built a life together, miserable as it was at times. I couldn't just walk away without a fight.

Besides, Terry was technically my boss, now. I'd been assigned to his project team. We'd spent the summer preparing for next year's ledger conversion and our interaction had been strictly professional.

Well... mostly, professional.

We'd been working together four months. There'd been a number of lunches, with larger groups, of course. A few happy hours. And that one night we were the last two working. He'd walked me to my car.

Nothing happened, but I could feel his eyes linger when I left a room. And warmth often flooded my belly at the sound of his voice. So, yeah. Maybe there was a small attraction. Big deal. I was with Collin, and Terry was dating some Whitney girl from his softball team. There could never be anything between us. How would that even work?

Still... "Alright, fine. What did he say?"

Heidi grinned like a schoolgirl. She whipped her head around, blonde curls flying. "Well," she said, conspiratorially, "according to Jordan in HR, Carla from disbursements ran into Terry at The Wharf Rat with that girl. You know, the one from his coed sports thing?" I nodded as she leaned closer and lowered her voice. "Anyway, Carla told Jordan they got to talking and he mentioned you like five times. Wanted to know your situation. What you're into. How long you've been with Collin. Stuff like that."

I made a dismissive sound. "I wouldn't believe anything Carla says." But pleasure burned like a torch in my chest. A torch that quickly defused.

Harmless speculation was one thing, but I had no right entertaining real thoughts about another guy. Especially when that guy had kind, gentle eyes that made me long for something more.

I sighed. Even if things were to end with Collin, it would take months to unravel. Terry would probably lose interest by then anyway. If he even was interested.

Which, he wasn't.

Fate Is a Fickle Beast

Terry

I could barely hear over the raucous cheering.

Jamie and I were watching the Redskins at a bar near his home in St. Mary's. I was down visiting my parents for Thanksgiving, and he and I were catching up. But my mind was in Baltimore.

"I can't stop thinking about her," I shouted over the noise.

Jamie groaned, draining the last of his beer. "So, quit whining and do something about it."

"What am I supposed to do? She's with someone, and she works for me."

This last part was only technically true. I had oversight of Steph's team, but she wasn't a direct report. Our dating would've been frowned upon, but not grounds for dismissal. Still a risk, though.

"You've been talking about this girl for like six months, now. Either make a move or move on. Life's too short." He signaled the bartender for another round. "You're in the city, right? Aren't there girls everywhere? Find someone else."

Easier said than done.

And I'd tried. But the more time I spent with Steph, the more I liked her. There was chemistry between us, not just attraction—but something deeper. And I wanted more.

I actually looked forward to work because of her. She saw the best in people. Brought optimism wherever she went. I even admired her determination to work things out with Collin, futile as that seemed. It was clear the guy didn't love her or take care of her in the way she deserved.

I wanted the chance to do those things. Take away the pain she felt. Show her there was more to love than this. Only fear was holding me back.

The Redskins scored, taking the lead for the first time, and another round of cheers rippled through the crowded bar. "I guess you're right," I told Jamie, sighing. "Maybe fate just isn't on my side."

But fate is a fickle beast.

Christmas fell several weeks after that Redskin game, as did the annual office celebration. This year, the head of finance was hosting at her home, and all were encouraged to bring their significant other.

I'd taken Jamie's advice and had reconnected with Whitney, a friend from softball who I'd dated briefly over the summer. There was no spark, but we had fun together and she'd agreed to come to the party with me.

What I did not consider was the possibility we'd arrive at the same time as Steph and Collin. Nor did I give much thought to how difficult it would be, seeing them together all night. And I certainly didn't count on the blood boiling anger I'd feel every time he criticized her—which was often.

Even Whitney was put off.

"What is that guy's problem?" she whispered after Steph missed a shot in the corner pocket and he made some cutting remark. A group of us were gathered in the basement playing a friendly game of pool, and he had nothing but insults.

She looked up at one point, flush with embarrassment, her sad-sweet eyes welling with tears. It took every ounce of self-control not to clock the guy. And by the end of the game, I was buzzed with fury and so much pent-up frustration, I couldn't hold back.

"Why don't you go find someone else to pick on?" I practically growled as he bent to rack up for the next game. "Or better yet, why don't you just leave."

A tense silence fell over the room as Collin straightened, his face hot with anger. All eyes were on him, and they weren't friendly eyes. We were family, and he'd hurt one of our own.

"Whatever," he said, after a moment's hesitation. He lifted the rack and balls scattered. "C'mon Steph. We're out of here."

He turned and strode from the room, confident she'd follow. Which, after a moment, she did. But I couldn't let it end that way.

It was now or never, and I was going to say my piece.

The Seinfeld Effect

Stephania

I was inches from the front door, ready to leave, when firm hands grasped my shoulders.

Terry's voice was low and close to my ear. "You don't have to go with him."

I paused, too stunned to argue, as he gently ushered me into a small room off to the side. Tears streamed down my cheeks, and I couldn't make them stop. Couldn't do anything but gaze up at his handsome face, now etched with concern and a raw determination I'd never seen.

It had been a miserable night. I hadn't planned on bringing Collin, but he'd insisted. We'd argued before coming, and he took every opportunity to undermine and embarrass me. It was mortifying.

And then... Terry.

I couldn't believe he called Collin out, right to his face! It was so... bold. So... unexpected... so... visceral. No one had ever stood up for me like that. Sure, they'd make little jabs about him in private, but Terry had the guts to defend me.

It was so...well, it was eye opening, for one thing. And, sexy as hell. And far too much for me to process. I felt dizzy with conflict even as I pulled away.

"What were you thinking? Why would you say something like that to him? He's going to be so angry."

There wasn't a shred of remorse on Terry's face. "Good. Let him. Someone had to do it." He crossed his arms and regarded me, his expression quickly softening. And there was such concern in his eyes. Such unmasked longing. "I care about you, Stephania. More than I have any right to—I realized that tonight. But even as a friend, I couldn't stand by and watch him treat you like that. This relationship is hurting you. Don't you see that?

I did.

But I'd become so accustomed to defending it, the words just rolled out. "It's not always like this. And you don't know Collin. He's had a lot going on with work. And we just—"

"—aren't good for each other," he finished. "And I think it's admirable, how you've tried to hang on. But you have to know he's not right for you. That's not what love should look like. And I think..." He paused, those kind, emerald eyes intense and searching. "No. I *know* that if you'd give me a chance, I could show you." He took my shaking hand in his. "I want to be the one to show you."

My heart squeezed with joy. I wanted that too. But then Collin's voice cut through the air, impatient and agitated, calling for me. The sound of him, like a slap of reality.

Could I really just walk away? I knew, despite our problems, he cared for me. We'd been together so long; I wasn't sure who I was apart from him. And Terry. What if it didn't work out? I'd be alone.

I shook my head, aching to throw my arms around him. To tell him, *Yes, I want you, too*. But who was I kidding? I didn't have the guts to leave. Maybe I never would. Anger and self-loathing roiled in my chest at the thought.

"What are you even saying, Terry? I can't just leave him, and you're here with—"

"I'm saying that I care about you. And I don't want to see you hurt. And the last thing I want is to come between you and him, but," he released my hand, his eyes still holding, "if you ever get to a point where you're done trying and want to move on? I'm here."

And then he kissed my forehead, and he was gone.

Things got bad after that. At home. At work. I was in a state of constant turmoil, caught in a web of guilt and conflicting desires. Like Terry, I knew, given the chance, we'd be good together. And I wanted him. I also wanted to do right by Collin and honor the promises we'd made. But was it right to stay when neither of us really loved each other? It seemed, there was no choice that didn't end in harm.

And so, I lingered in the middle. And I might've stayed there. For years, maybe, if it hadn't been for Jerry Seinfeld.

The comedian was in Baltimore that spring performing stand up, and someone at work had secured a row of sought-after seats. I knew Terry was going. He tried to distance himself after the party, but we remained close. Our interaction, though mostly work related, was fraught with meaningful eye contact, loaded phrases, and the not-so-innocent brushing of limbs.

I couldn't deny how much I wanted him, and the pain of attraction was almost unbearable. The guilt, however, was agonizing. As was my decision to see the show. Collin was a fan, and I knew he'd want to go. I also knew I'd rather die than sit in a theatre between him and Terry.

"Tell him the tickets are for employees only," Heidi suggested when I shared this dilemma. A solution that backfired, as it turned out, because he made alternative plans for us that night. A ruse, to keep me from going without him.

Which is how I found myself lying, the night of the show, about working late, and fake laughing through Seinfeld's routine to cover the anxious pit in my stomach. I'm not sure why I felt so driven to be there, but in hindsight, I know it was fate.

At one point during Seinfeld's routine, I'd looked over at Terry, who smiled, his face relaxed with enjoyment. And then, at Heidi and Steve, so happy together. At our other co-workers and their dates, laughing and carefree. I wanted what they had. Wanted to be here *with* Terry, as a couple.

I wanted more than this constant ball of anxiety I'd been carrying; guilt and consequence be damned.

And, bizarre as it sounds, with the words of Jerry Seinfeld ringing in my ears, I finally knew what I had to do.

It Started with a Piss

Terry

The months following the concert were the longest of my life.

Weeks after attending Jerry Seinfeld's show, Steph and Collin split for good. On Heidi's advice, I kept my distance. They'd been together a long time and it hadn't been an easy decision.

Besides, I didn't want to be her rebound guy, I wanted a chance at something real. So, I took a painful step back. Dated Whitney a handful of times, went on vacation with a buddy of mine from home. All the while, waiting.

Hoping... when Steph was ready, she'd choose me.

And on the eve of the summer solstice, my patience paid off.

"Shopping?" Jamie groaned on his end of the line. "You're kidding me, right? You've waited a year to date this girl and you're taking her shopping?" He chuckled. "Sounds kind of lame."

I grinned into the phone. Lame or not, nothing could dampen my mood today. Steph would be here any minute, and that's all that mattered.

"Well, I think it's romantic," I told him.

I'll admit, shopping at a home furnishing store wasn't your average first date. But it suited us. I'd needed a few things for the house, and, as I was hoping she'd be part of my future, I figured, why not include her from the start?

Future.

I grinned at the word. It had never felt so bright. I hung up with Jamie and made a final sweep of the house.

Steph had spent the last several months recovering from the break with Collin. It hadn't been easy, but the strength and courage she'd shown, standing on her own two feet, and taking her life back, made me want her even more.

When she mentioned she was free this weekend, I'd jumped at the chance. She'd known I was furnishing the house and had been excited to help. Besides, we knew each other better than awkward meals and packed movie theaters. After all this waiting, we just wanted to be together.

The doorbell rang, and I almost tripped in my haste to answer, swinging the door wide with a grin. There she was— shining black curls and a shy smile.

She took a step forward and closed the door, and then we were alone, at last. I pulled her into a warm hug, loving her sweet scent, and the effortless way our bodies fit together.

"Hi," she said, her voice muffled against my chest.

I swept my fingers through her hair. "Hi, yourself. Have any trouble getting here?"

She shook her head, then pulled back to look at me with no hesitation in her smile. This was right, and we both knew it. "Can you believe this is really happening? It feels like a dream."

"A dream come true," I said.

My face grew hot as she sputtered with laughter at the corny line, but I didn't care. It was true, and we were finally together, and that was all that mattered.

We never did make it to Pier One that day. In fact, we never left my house. We sat on the couch and talked for hours, finally free to share the thoughts and feelings we'd held back for so long.

Within weeks, we committed to each other. And, after a whirlwind year of sneaking around at work, exotic trips, endless laughter, and more love than any heart deserves, I knew I'd found my soulmate. It was time to take the final step.

Marriage.

But first, the proposal.

I'm kind of an old-fashioned guy, so getting Steph's dad's blessing was important to me. I'm also painfully shy, and thoughts of that conversation gave me the cold sweats. I put it off for weeks.

My opportunity finally came at a most unexpected time. In the most unexpected of places—a crowded restroom in a strip shopping mall.

Steph and I had been heading to see a movie when we ran into her parents. They decided to join us, and we all went for ice cream after, chatting amicably about the film—a romantic comedy. It was a fun night, and I decided, should the opportunity present itself, I'd approach her dad.

Toward the end of the evening, I found myself standing behind him in a lengthy line, waiting for the men's room. *Just do it,* a little voice urged inside me, *What's the worst thing that can happen?*

I leaned close to his ear.

"Sir, I know this isn't the best place to do this. But I really love your daughter. And I want to marry her. I've been trying to work up the courage for a month now to ask you..." My heart was slamming into my chest as I choked out the final words. "Would you please give me your blessing to marry Stephania?"

And then I exhaled the world's longest breath and waited.

Unfortunately, two side by side urinals opened at that same moment, and, as there was a line, we had no choice but to advance.

Believe me when I say, it was the most awkward piss I've ever taken.

We washed hands and exited in silence as my panic grew. Steph's dad liked me; I was certain of it. Hadn't even considered he might say no. Or, worse yet, nothing.

What could that mean?

Sweat beaded at my brow. Once we rounded the corner, Steph and her mom would be waiting. What would I do then?

Was it possible he didn't hear me?

Thankfully, at the end of the hallway he paused, pulling me aside with a look of amusement. He smiled warmly.

"You caught me off guard back there," he said, taking my hand firmly in his. "Of course, you have my blessing. You've made Steph happier than I've ever seen her, and I'd be honored to call you son. Welcome to the family, Terry."

Epilogue

Stephania

And that's how it started.

A wedding, a too-tight skirt, Jerry Seinfeld, and an awkward moment at the urinal.

Four kids, three houses, and two decades later, we are still together. Still laughing. Still making each other's dreams come true.

Terry proposed the week after seeking my dad's blessing. He surprised me with a simple, yet romantic candlelit dinner, complete with piano music and the most gorgeous ring I'd ever laid eyes on. He knelt before me with endless oceans of love twinkling in those emerald eyes, and the promise of a heart, devoted.

Though initially we kept the relationship secret, in time our colleagues and supervisors lent their full support. They even threw us a surprise wedding shower!

Jamie and Terry have remained close. He and Megan were among the first of Terry's friends I met after we started dating. Tales of their legendary wedding weekend, and Terry's... um... inebriation, are still spoken of.

Heidi and Steve are married, too. The four of us have stayed good friends. For a time, we sat in a row together— me, Heidi, Terry, and Steve. *Lover's Lane*, some called it. There was another nickname, which I won't relay, but those who were there know. We had a lot of nicknames back then. A lot of fun, too. I wish there was time to recount it all.

So many kind souls were part of our story. I will always carry pieces of them with me. Those days in the trenches hold some of my fondest memories. With some of my favorite people.

One of whom, I'm blessed to share a life with.

Someday

by Diana Dubs

When I was nineteen years old, I promised myself I would never date someone in the military. *Ever*. For multiple reasons. I couldn't do long distance again, not after my last relationship. I was selfish. I had dreams. I had plans. I appreciated that the military served and protected us, but I knew I couldn't do it. I couldn't be a navy girlfriend or a military wife or whatever the title was.

I like to think that God laughed when I made that promise. Good-naturedly, of course. *Challenge accepted, Diana.* Because what I didn't know at nineteen years old, what I couldn't have guessed, is that ten years later, an army officer would kneel on the rocky shores of Lake Ontario and propose to me.

And I would say yes.

The story of our engagement is multi-layered and woven over five years; it's a single moment built upon thousands of moments merged together. It's a story of love and forgiveness, of trial and error, of laughter and silliness, but most of all, our story is about two people who chose each other, time and time again, no matter what.

The very first choice was when his profile popped up on Coffee Meets Bagel, my dating app. In the middle of cooking dinner, as I headed to my bedroom to put on fluffy socks, I remembered to check the dating app for my daily "bagel," and I stopped dead in the hallway.

A sandy-haired, brown-eyed, dimpled guy grinned from an airplane cockpit, his arm resting casually on the seat beside him as if to say, *you should be sitting here.* It wasn't cocky or arrogant, but warm, inviting.

It's shallow, but he was incredibly good-looking.

Forgetting about dinner, I scrolled through the rest of the photos and read Derek's profile.

I am shy when you first meet me, but love to socialize when I become comfortable.

Me too!

I appreciate when my date shows subtle affection and enjoys the company of my friends as well as alone time.

I like that. Totally fine with that.

I hesitated for a moment when I read Derek had served in the army and was now at West Point.

But what did I have to lose? Nothing. Odds were low. None of my other conversations had amounted to anything, so what was the chance that this one would?

Despite the fact that he was a cadet at West Point, the United States Military Academy, and despite the promise my younger self had made, I clicked "connect" without a flicker of fear.

You never know, right?

Like any other dating app or service, Coffee Meets Bagel begins with simply messaging back and forth. Its unique feature is that the chat room closes after a week, which forces people to exchange numbers or meet in person. After a few weeks of "casually" texting—reading Derek's message, waiting an odd number of minutes, like seven or eight, then carefully crafting a response, then putting my phone down and walking away—he texted me and asked if I wanted to go flying with him. He had his fixed wing license, and he regularly flew at a local airport as part of West Point's flying team.

On an unrelated note, would you like to go flying with me? Derek texted. *I have plans to go flying on Saturday and thought you might want to come along.*

I didn't hesitate. *I'd love to.*

To me, the answer was obvious—of course I said yes. I was twenty-three years old, and while I wanted the Big Picture Love, I wasn't expecting to find it any time soon. I just always assumed I'd be older when I found The One, and until then, why not have some adventure and excitement? Not to say I'd date just anyone. I had my standards. I wanted to date someone who was simply good, someone who fully accepted who I was, who was passionate about his own dreams and independent enough to handle mine.

From the moment I met Derek, I knew a good man stood before me. Even though I had never met him before, I'd be perfectly safe going flying with him.

Derek still can't believe I said yes.

Derek was easy to fall in love with. It was one of those sweet smooth slides, as simple and effortless as the sun shining on a summer day. He was goofy; he was smart; he was affectionate. We balanced each other out: I was Type A; Derek was Type B. When my grandfather died, Derek was there for me in a way I had never experienced before.

We were young, twenty-three years old, and our careers were laid out before us. Derek still had a year left at West Point, followed by a year (or two) of flight school in Alabama, and then at least five more years on his military contract. For me, I was going to earn tenure at my school district, which was still three years away, and I had already started working on my master's degree for literacy. If we wanted to follow our dreams and be together, long-distance was the only option for the next couple of years.

I wanted to laugh and cry when I remembered that promise I had once made.

We believed in *someday* for us. Someday, we could be a "normal" couple. Someday, we could live together.

We believed if we made a life together, we would be happy.

There was a future for us, and we believed in it.

The truth is, I was reminded of that promise to myself over and over again. Long-distance has a way of making you question everything. The first year and a half of our relationship, which occurred while Derek was still at West Point, was smooth sailing. It was easy to believe in that future when life was so good between us. But when Derek left for Alabama, that's when the reality sunk in. I was twenty-five years old. It was time to seriously acknowledge where this was going or leave the relationship, something Derek and I had always agreed on. If there wasn't a future in the relationship, what was the point of continuing it? There were only ever two options: break up, or get married.

But how did I know I wanted to get married to Derek?

I'd have to move. People might think that teaching is the ideal career for a military spouse, since all states need teachers, but it's not that easy. Not only are there are different certifications with every state, but it's not an easy job to pick up and start over. Teachers flourish when they have the chance to nurture their craft and hone their curriculum over time. A new grade, a new school, is essentially starting all over again. I loved teaching. When it came to being a teacher, I had all I ever wanted right in the palm of my hand. How could I just give that up for some guy?

For another year and a half, we saw each other about every six weeks, which was pretty good considering how difficult it was to fly to Alabama, and when we were together, we were happy. It was when we were apart that I questioned everything. I wanted us to actually commit, to acknowledge what we wanted from our relationship, but the truth was, neither one of us was ready to. There's no reason for it, and neither one of was a "bad" guy for it, either. We simply just weren't ready.

Our relationship survived only by choosing each other again and again and believing in someday. No matter how tough it got, no matter how far away it seemed, one of us always believed in someday, and it kept our love together.

After Alabama, Derek was stationed at Fort Drum, located in northern New York, and we began a year of "short distance." A four-hour car ride was nothing compared to Alabama, and all those questions and concerns I had stopped mattering.

What about your teaching career?

What about it? I can teach anywhere I go, and maybe I'd like some time to try something else. Write full-time. I always thought I'd be a stay-at-home mom, anyway.

What about picking up and relocating all the time?

What about it? Home is where your heart is, and what I learned from those weekends, is that we could make a home together anywhere.

How do you know if you'll be happy? Or you won't regret it?

The last one was almost laughable.

When we learned Derek would deploy in the fall of 2019, the plan was simple. I would stay at my job, in my town, in the same apartment I had for the last five years. It would be one last year there, a year to enjoy my tenure status, and then I'd relocate.

There was never a moment when everything hit me that yes, Derek was it. This was going to be the person I spent the rest of my life with. Deployment simply changed everything. When your loved one is halfway around the world and your relationship only grows stronger (despite a global pandemic) there's just nothing else that can compare.

Five years after we met, years of choosing each other time and time again, Derek and I were finally living together in a town outside of Fort Drum and ready to start our next chapter. Together.

I had finally accepted what being in a military relationship would mean for my job and my life, and I was both at peace and excited. To my complete surprise, I had landed a wonderful teaching job soon after relocating, which was even better! I had just assumed I wouldn't be able to find a teaching job since that would be a worst-case scenario, but that was silly of me to assume that. We created a five-year plan based on Derek's military timeline—two years left at Fort Drum (which would be the perfect time to get married), then a brief six months for a training course (the perfect time to start a family) then relocate to another post for about three years (then figure it out from there).

If we wanted to get married before we left New York, then Derek needed to propose, and soon. It would take us at least a year to plan and prepare for the wedding, and the military had given us a deadline.

School began.

Derek told me he had started looking for rings.

We dressed as Joe Exotic and a tiger for Halloween.

A close friend of mine became engaged. I thought I'd be engaged first, but I was not.

Thanksgiving happened.

On his birthday, he told me that he wished for something about us, but he didn't want to tell me in case it didn't come true.

Christmas passed.

Derek is an all or nothing kind of guy. When it comes to shopping, it's either an impulse buy, or he spends hours meticulously researching the product before making a decision. I had no doubts: Derek would not settle when it came to finding an engagement ring. He knew my general criteria (pear shape diamond with a unique band), but he admitted he hadn't found anything he loved. To be fair, the few times I searched on Zales' or Kay's websites, I hadn't found anything else I liked, either.

In January, I decided a direct course of action was needed, especially since he would be leaving soon for a six-week training. On a dreary Sunday afternoon, while we were tucked in our cozy living room, I made my move.

Derek stretched out in our soft gray recliner. Approaching from behind the chair, I pressed my check to his and slid my phone in his face. "Look at these," I said, showing him the Brilliant Earth search results. Their rings were ethically sourced, and they had more ring options than any other jewelry company I'd stumbled across. "I like basically everything on this page."

"Wow." Derek scrolled down the page. "I really like a lot of these."

My heart leapt. "I do, too. Which ones?"

After we considered some of the engagement rings, I took the next step. "Should I pick out some of my favorites?"

Derek smiled my favorite smile. The smile that's just for me, the one that's soft and full of love and this undeniable warmth in those sweet brown eyes. "Yeah. Pick out your favorites."

So, I did. I chose three. My favorite was called the Tiara. It had a patterned band, alternating between marquise and circular diamonds. I loved how intricate it looked, but I also adored a twist band with two side stones. One of the twists sparkled with tiny diamonds. The third was simpler, a plain band with embellishments on either side of the main diamond, but it would be gorgeous with a more intricate wedding band. Somewhere, whether it be in the engagement ring or wedding band, I wanted something intricate and patterned. Something no one else had or could easily find. Just like Derek.

Just like me.

Derek left for a six-week training, as military life dictates, and I spent those weeks trying not to wonder if he ordered it and if I made a mistake. Six weeks of looking at pictures of the engagement rings and then trying to distract myself. The more I looked at pictures of the twisted band with the three diamonds, the more I liked. Should I tell Derek I wanted the twisted band and not the Tiara?

Ultimately, I decided not to say anything.

When Derek returned from the training, I couldn't help myself. I had to know if he had made a decision. "Do you know what ring you want to get?"

"I think so. Do you want to guess?"

"No, no. I want to be surprised." Not just surprised, but I wanted the final choice to be up to him.

In early March, I came home from a long-overdue haircut as Derek returned from work.

"I have a phone meeting tonight," he told me and wrestled his boots off in the hallway.

"No prob—"

"It's a ring meeting," he blurted. "For your ring. I have an appointment to pick your engagement ring."

I laughed. It was classic Derek—honest to a fault and too impatient for surprises. He headed upstairs to our office, making sure to shut the door. Downstairs in the kitchen, I couldn't stop smiling as I made dinner, a creamy penne and chicken dish from HelloFresh.

Maybe other girls would be bothered that they knew, but I relished it. There was something comforting about knowing it was happening. For so long in our relationship, I hadn't known. Long distance had a way of making you question your relationship and your life, and to have reached the place of peace, of knowing true contentment with your loved one... it was like being introduced to my forever home.

When Derek nonchalantly strolled into the living room, picked up his wallet, and headed back upstairs, I laughed. Of course, he'd forgotten his wallet downstairs.

So, I knew the ring was ordered. I began scheduling biweekly manicures. The ring wasn't in yet, obviously, but my nails were going to be ready, just like how I'd always dreamed as a teenager. When I was proposed to in the far-off someday, my nails were going to be perfect.

I knew when Derek spoke to my father because, frustrated with himself, Derek kept telling me all the opportunities he missed to speak with him. We had traveled to my parents' beach house for a few days on my spring break. Derek had plenty of opportunities—when I went for a run in the morning, when I offered to go back and grab my mom's jacket when she forgot it. Derek confessed each time he missed his chance. Finally, on our last afternoon sitting on the beach, my mom and I headed to the house to use the bathroom and left Derek and Dad alone.

Derek said nothing about missing the opportunity, therefore, I knew he didn't.

I knew when the ring arrived because I was the only one home when it came and it needed to be signed for. I thrust it in the closet and ran into the kitchen, wondering if I would be able to forget that the diamond ring I would wear for the rest of my life was six feet away in a cardboard box, sitting on a filing cabinet. I began reading a book and promptly put it out of my mind.

Someday

I knew we would be engaged before April 24th because we discussed being engaged at my brother's wedding.

And on a Tuesday, two weeks before my brother's wedding, when Derek suggested we go for brunch and a walk for the upcoming weekend, I knew that would be the moment.

On Friday night, I looked for signs that Derek was nervous. It was a quiet Friday for us, something we enjoyed, take-out from Chipotle and a movie. Derek was completely normal with one exception: he insisted we go to bed early. Derek is the definition of a night-owl. The later, the better. I'm the one who falls asleep on our green chaise couch, wakes up, and then groggily insists we go to bed. "We have to be up early," he explained. "I don't want us to be cranky."

This was true. It wasn't our regular weekend brunch. It was Tin Pan's reopening weekend. The restaurant had closed down during the pandemic and was rumored to never open again. Now, it was back under new ownership, and Derek and I were going for brunch for the very first time. Two years ago, before Derek deployed, we had eaten dinner there with his parents, but we hadn't realized its brunch reputations. My new coworkers reminisced about its famed stuffed French toast, while another military friend solemnly swore it had the best biscuits and gravy in the entire country. I had heard from another local that the brunch line would wind down the entire street on Sunday mornings. Tin Pan didn't take brunch reservations, and considering Tin Pan's reputation, we knew if we wanted a spot, we had to get there early.

"I hope it doesn't rain," Derek said as we drove into town. It was a murky, cloudy day, the kind where the clouds are too bright, like they haven't made up their minds about if they want to rain or not.

"Me too."

By the time we arrived, a short line had formed. I hopped out as Derek parked on the other side of the street. Together, we waited in line, hand in hand, on the sidewalk. Derek craned his neck to check the sky, and when he met my eyes, he smiled. Neither one of us spoke as more people joined the cue, and then Derek claimed he forgot something in the car and headed back across the street, and I wondered if he was grabbing the ring.

We didn't have to wait long.

It was a perfectly lovely and ordinary brunch, complete with crème brulé French toast, a side of sausage, and mimosas. It was legendary.

Then, it was time for our walk.

Sackets Harbor is located on the edge of Lake Ontario. In the spring, it was a picturesque postcard—restored red brick buildings dripped with ivy, baskets of bright flowers dangled from the black iron lamp posts. Local restaurants and shops lined the main street, and a grand white bandstand overlooked a small park and harborside walkway. In the summer, boats and jet skis docked alongside it.

At the end of the main street, there was a small museum, and then, the battlefield from the War of 1812. High above the water, the battlefield was a wide expanse of lush green with a walkway weaving along the outer edge. A few trees dotted the battlefield; a gray memorial commemorated the heart of it, and a stone wall protected anyone from tumbling down the rocky cliff to the lake. Despite its history, it was a peaceful place, a beautiful one.

My heart kicked up as we approached the museum, which marked the entrance to the battlefield. This had to be it. Somewhere on the battlefield, with the water and the sky as our witness, Derek was going to get on one knee and propose.

Instead of leading me to the walkway, Derek paused. The gate behind the museum was open.

Nothing intrigued Derek so much as adventure. "Can we explore?" he asked, squeezing my hand. "I want to know where it goes."

"Sure." I tried to keep my voice calm, but excitement and nerves buzzed through my brains, my heart. With every step, we were getting closer to the moment itself.

Neither of us had ever been to the museum before. We followed the path through the gate, which led us through the museum's backyard, down the hill past a barn, and onto the rocky shore of Lake Ontario itself.

It was like stepping into a snow globe. There was no beach, just a map of flat, broken rocks and round stones. Water gently lapped at the rocks, and the murky clouds had drifted away, leaving a sun shining in a blue sky. Surrounded by only the water and the sky, the world was wide around us, full of possibility.

It was breathtaking.

"Hold on," Derek said, heading towards the huge lilac bush behind us. I stifled a grin. The public bathrooms we had passed were locked.

I breathed in the crisp lake-scented air. Would he have our friends take our picture? I didn't think so. It was so empty, surely, I would have seen one of them hanging around. Would I cry? Would he cry?

Derek rejoined me, and we were closer than ever.

I turned around to take a picture, careful not to capture my shadow in the photo. Would Derek be on one knee when I turned around? Something told me he would be. After all, if this was a movie, it would be the perfect moment.

He was not.

Disappointed, I stowed my phone in my bag, and then Derek spoke.

"Well," he said. "In true Derek fashion, this wasn't where I planned, but it's perfect, and I'm going with it."

He kneeled down. I tried to take it all in. I tried to memorize it like a painting—each brush stroke of emotion, the color of every word, the frame of the moment. I wanted to remember this for the rest of my life, the moment I had waited so long for.

When Derek opened the ring box, I promptly forgot everything.

It was the surprise I hadn't expected—the twisted band with three stones, sparkling brilliantly against the blue water and the blue sky, nothing but love from Derek.

To this day, I still don't fully remember this moment. It's probably shock, which I never expected. Even though I was completely aware of what was going on, somehow, I was still in a state of shock. I remember the rest of the day very clearly, even what happened after I said yes, but this moment is fragmented into bits and pieces. For some reason, I can't piece them together in order. I know he mentioned talking to my father; I know my legs trembled; I know I thought I might cry. I don't know if Derek opened the ring box right away or at the end of his proposal.

What I remember the most, in crystallizing clarity, is the moment I saw the ring nestled in against the black velvet.

Not the Tiara band after all, but the one with three stones and the twisted band.

Derek knows me better than I know myself.

Even though I had never told him the twisted band was my favorite, he knew that was the one I would want.

I threw my head back (I think), held my left hand out, and said yes.

That was our moment. It was quick. The photo before the proposal and the first picture of the ring were only minutes apart.

I tell Derek almost every single day that I love my ring. I take it off to shower or wash the dishes, and afterwards, I usually present it to Derek. He takes it with a grin, says, "Lucky me," and slides it back where it belongs on my left hand.

It's been said an engagement ring with three stones represents the past, the present, and the future.

When I was nineteen, I thought dating someone in the military meant that it completely defined you. It doesn't.

When I met Derek, I thought we could be really happy together, but I was afraid of what the risks would be.

When we hit our rocky patches, I thought of *someday*, and it kept us going.

When Derek proposed, *someday* had already started.

I'm twenty-nine. I live in a cozy little townhouse with a collage of our belongings and furniture. I smile when I go to work each day because I feel like I'm living in a Nora Roberts novel—the spunky and likeable heroine, enjoying the everyday of her quaint town, falling in love (with the exception of the serial killers or elements of danger Roberts is so fond of).

I'm going to marry the love of my life, Derek, who just happens to be serving in the army. I'm not defined by his job, nor will our marriage be.

I have my *someday* today, and as my sparkling ring reminds me, I'll have it in the future, too.

Just My Bill

by Paul Iasevoli

In 1982, Thursdays at the Mach 5 were anything-goes, buy-one-get-one free nights. It was the one weeknight when straight punk rockers, drag queens, and feathery or leathery gay men and women could congregate in a strip-mall bar just off the shore of Lake Ronkonkoma. In those days, that area of Central Long Island was not the most liberal part of the New York City region, but on the night before the weekend, the Mach 5 was filled to capacity, and I was one of their "star" dancers. Which meant, I made a spectacle of myself until the place closed at two a.m., pogoing and twirling to the tunes of Blondie and The Cars until I was drenched in sweat. Although I was a star on the dance floor, I went home alone almost every night—at twenty-three, I longed for adult stability.

It was mid-July when I met my other. The contract for my first year's teaching assignment at the Middle Island School for Emotionally Disturbed Children had ended, and I was living on my seventy-five dollar a week unemployment checks—just enough to pay some rent to my parents to live in their summer house in West Hampton, with a little left over for gas, and a cheap night out with friends.

The Mach 5 was packed that Thursday night. I stood elbow to elbow with my friend, Pete, and his latest conquest.

"You got money on you?" I asked.

Pete scowled. "You broke again?"

I nodded.

"How much?"

"Ten bucks?"

"What for?"

I pointed to a hot blond across the bar. "You see that guy?"

Pete squinted. "What about him?"

"I need to meet him."

"You need to meet him?" Pete shook his head. "But you'll need to pay me back."

"Yeah, but can you wait till Tuesday?"

Pete sighed and handed me a ten-dollar bill. I kissed him on the cheek. "I'll pay you back next Tuesday...maybe."

"*This Tuesday*," Pete said.

I nodded as he walked out of the Mach 5 with his trick for the night in tow.

I turned back to my prospect. His blue eyes and blond hair were the perfect combination to fit my bill for a William Shatner-Captain Kirk fantasy—all my schoolboy dreams in one tight package. I leaned across the bar and waved the ten-dollar bill Pete had lent me at the bartender. He spotted my urgency and hustled over. "A drink, good lookin'?"

I cast my gaze at the bar well. "What'd you got at half price?"

The bartender scratched his head. "Happy hour's over."

I held up the ten. "This is all I got."

He winked, took the bill, and passed me two Scotch and sodas. "That'll be five."

"Five?"

The bartender nodded. "Two-fifty for you and two-fifty for the drink you're buyin' for Billy Actor...the guy you're eyein' across the way."

"Billy Actor?" I asked.

The bartender gave me a wink and nodded. "Fella, I've been doin' this for too many years to not notice what's goin' on—you and Billy Actor have got the connect. I'll send the drink over to him and tell him it's from you—so go 'round the other side of the bar and talk to him. Just 'cause he looks like Captain Kirk, don't mean he's not approachable...go... talk to him."

I took a long sip of my Scotch and let the Dutch courage the bartender poured kick in. Once it did, I sauntered to the other side of the bar to talk to the guy the barkeep called "Billy Actor."

I stopped short before I got close to him—his broad shoulders and thin waist took my breath away. He turned and smiled, raised the Scotch and soda I'd bought him to his lips, took a sip, and motioned for me to join him. I hesitated at his come-on, but his sparkling blue eyes were all I needed to accept his invitation to strike up a conversation that might lead to more than a one-night stand.

I took another gulp of my Scotch-Dutch courage and extended my hand. "I'm Paul." He took my hand in his and squeezed with a grip neither firm nor hard, but with a gentleness that gave me confidence that I could get to know him better.

"Bill," he said.

I shifted my gaze from his and looked down at the floor. "The bartender told me your name was Billy...Billy Actor.

He threw his head back and chuckled. "That's what they call me around this place, but I'm just Bill...like the song from *Show Boat*."

"Huh?"

"The musical...*Show Boat*? Don't you know it?"

I took another sip of my drink. "Oh. Yeah, sure," I lied.

Bill stared at me. "You gay?"

"What?"

"Are you gay? What kind of fag don't know songs from musical theater?"

"Um...this one?"

Bill grinned and pointed to the stool next to him. "Sit down."

I squeezed in beside him so closely that our thighs rubbed together. As The Circle Jerks pulsated from the DJ booth, Keith Morris's screeching about not living past thirty squelched any conversation Bill and I attempted. Once the tumultuous pounding stopped, and the sweaty punkers filed off the dance floor, the DJ switched the mood to a tranquil mix of the Police's "Walking on the Moon."

"I love this song," I said.

Bill nodded. "Yeah, a little less angry than The Circle Jerks. You want to dance?"

I swallowed the dregs of my Scotch and soda, got off the barstool, and took Bill's hand. I felt as if I were floating, as I skipped down the three stairs leading to the small dance floor. The DJ switched the lighting from the flashing red of the previous song to an undulating blue-green that enhanced the rhythms of Sting's melodic vocals. As the opening chords vibrated, Bill pulled me close. "I was staring at you from when you walked in, you know."

I did a little dance twirl away from him; he pulled me back and pressed himself against me so tightly I could feel his heart beat next to mine. "I know," I muttered.

He rocked with me through the hook of the song, and I let myself meld with him in four-four time. When the instrumental picked up again, he asked, "Who's the guy you walked in with?"

"The guy I walked in with...Pete?"

"Yeah. Is he your boyfriend?"

"He's my friend and a boy..."

"And he gave you money before he left."

"Oh, that...that was...that was so I had ten bucks to hang out a little longer...longer to meet *you*."

The final cymbals of the Police tune reverberated, and Bill pressed his lips to mine. My mouth opened wide. I let his warm breath mingle with mine, and it was as if a crescendo ran from the soles of my feet to the top of my head.

When Phill Collins' "In the Air Tonight" played signaling that the Mach 5's two a.m. closing time was near, Bill wrapped his arms around my shoulders and drew me closer. He put his mouth next to my ear. "You want to get out of here and go somewhere else?"

His warm breath tingled down my neck so much so that I had no choice but to say yes to his request. He tugged my hand and led me out the door. In the parking lot the July heat and humidity rose from the pavement making the wee morning hours seem blithe with foggy vapors.

"My car's over there." Bill pointed to a blue Valiant across the way.

I thought about my other almost-one-nightstands that had gone bad in car backseats and shook my head. "If we're going to go somewhere else," I said, "I'd rather drive myself."

Bill's eyes narrowed. "You're not very trusting, are you?"

I shrugged. "It's not that...it's just...just that my mother told me never to get into cars with strangers."

Bill guffawed. "Strangers? Do you always let strangers kiss you on the dance floor?"

I had to laugh in spite of myself. "Not too often," I said. "Where'd you have in mind to go? It's after two in the morning. What's open until four a.m. on Long Island on a weeknight?"

"La Bise." Bill pointed across the lake.

"Huh?"

"La Bise used to be the Swiss Inn. A guy from upstate bought it and made it into a gay getaway for the overflow crowd from Fire Island. It's only open in the summer and has a really nice piano bar. I worked there last season serving drinks and singing. I was their singing waiter. I got to keep my tips, but the owners never paid me a salary." Bill tugged at my elbow to lead me toward his car.

I froze. "Wait...I can't."

He turned and stopped in the middle of the hot pavement. "You can't what?"

"I can't go." I stared at the ground. "I ain't got no money left."

"Money? You're worried about money? Don't worry, they never make me pay in that place."

I shrugged. "Yeah...but...I only got five dollars."

Bill grimaced. "Rawmaish! You don't need money."

"Rawmaish." I laughed. "What the fuckity fuck does that mean?"

"'Rawmaish?' It's what my Irish grandmother used to say—it means something like 'bullshit.'"

"Rawmaish," I repeated and giggled. "But I'm driving myself." I pointed to my white Gran Prix a few spaces away from Bill's blue Valiant.

"Suit yourself." Bill headed to his car. "But follow me once I pull out of my space. The place is a little tricky to find, especially at night."

I waved him off and got into my car.

The winding road around Lake Ronkonkoma was dark and damp from the mists that came off the water in mid-July. I hadn't a clue as to where La Bise was, so I followed close behind Bill's Valiant. He drove a little too fast for me, and more than once I had to grip the steering wheel to keep from

HOW I MET MY OTHER

swerving into the trees that lined each side of the two lane we were on.

Ten minutes later the sulfur lights of La Bise reflected off the lake, and the chords of a piano accompanied by the voices of an off-key male chorus filtered on a whoosh of wind coming through my open driver's side window. Bill tapped his brakes twice and put on his directional to signal that we'd arrived at La Bise.

I made a sharp right into the parking lot and stopped short behind Bill's car, my tires kicking up gravel as I pulled into a space next to him.

He got out of his car and poked his face into my driver's side window. "You always drive like that?"

I stuck my tongue out at him as I turned off the engine. "It's *you* who drives like a crazy Italian," I said and stepped out of my car.

Bill put his hands on my shoulders and looked me up and down. "Get it right, I'm Irish. You're the Italian."

"How'd you know?"

"The black hair, bushy mustache, and wife-beater T-shirt might be a giveaway."

I nudged him hard and took his elbow as we walked toward the outdoor bar.

The doorman greeted Bill with a handshake. "Oh my God, as I live and breathe. We haven't seen you here in over a year. Where've you been?"

Bill shrugged. "Around."

The doorman shouted to the patrons at the bar and around the piano, "Billy Actor's here to grace us with his presence."

Bill glanced at me and turned his gaze back to the doorman. "Mikey, stop," he said and stuffed a ten-dollar bill in the doorman's hand.

Mikey tucked the ten back into Bill's cigarette pocket. "You're kiddin' me?" he said. "Billy Actor don't pay for nothin' in this joint...so long's you promise to give us a tune tonight."

Bill smirked. "It's nearly three a.m. I ain't no morning songbird."

"You hear that, fellas?" Mikey said over his shoulder, "Billy Actor ain't in the mood for singin' tonight."

Boos and raspberries rose up from the crowd. The piano player tapped out the first four notes of "Bill" from *Show Boat,* and the male chorus around the piano followed with the next six-note bar.

Bill ignored their stares and sidelong glances as they scanned me—a scantily clad, swarthy Italian in tow with a Captain-Kirk-looking Irishman who could sing. He led me over to the bar. The thin, red-haired, freckle-faced bartender extended his hand toward Bill. "Billy Actor. Long time no see."

Bill gripped the bartender's hand firm and hard. "Same here, Rusty."

The bartender pointed to me. "And what do we have there?" His eyes opened wide.

Bill pulled me closer to the bar. "Paul, Rusty; Rusty, Paul."

Rusty's freckles turned into one big blush as he shook my hand. "Well, why ain't we never seen *you* here before?"

I let Bill answer for me, "Because you just reopened for the season, and this is Paul's first time here."

"Oh, a virgin then?"

45

"Hardly," I said. "Well...almost hardly." I blushed knowing that heavy petting didn't count toward what Rusty was alluding to.

Rusty snickered. "That's like hardly being queer."

Bill put his arm around my shoulders. "Cut it out, Rusty and give us two Dewar's and soda."

Rusty poured the drinks and pushed them across the bar. Bill took the ten out of his cigarette pocket and handed it to Rusty, but Rusty pushed it back. "You know you don't pay in this place." Bill stuffed the ten into his pocket and led me over to the piano.

"What did you do, let everybody in this place screw you... so that now you don't have to pay for anything?"

Bill chuckled. "No...no, I was their biggest draw when they first opened. I dragged all my theater friends, gay and straight, here after shows. Then we'd sing for the patrons after hours—I suppose that makes me La Bise's star...as close as I'll ever get to stardom on Long Island." He pulled a stool out from the far side of the piano and motioned for me to sit down.

I settled into a spot at the wide curve of the piano and took a long swig of my drink. I gagged a little as I swallowed—the bartender had gone heavy on the Dewar's and light on the soda.

Bill slapped me between my shoulder blades. "You okay?"

I nodded. "Seems Rusty likes you...he poured our drinks with a heavy hand."

Bill grinned and sipped his Scotch.

The piano player—an older man with wavy, longish, pure-white hair—tinkered from tune to tune until he fixed his gaze on Bill. With a flourish he stood up, clapped his hands in the air to get the crowd's attention, and announced, "Tonight, gentlemen...and less gentle men..." Boos and cat-calls arose from the twenty or more guys gathered around the piano. "Tonight...tonight, we have the privilege of Billy Actor in our midst, and his lovely, young protégé—"

"Paul," I shouted.

"Paul," the piano player shouted back. "And Paul, what would you like to hear Billy sing?"

I looked up at Bill and took his hand in mine. "Sing 'Misty' for me." I chose that song only because I knew it from the movie, and I couldn't think of another tune that might fit the mood of La Bise at nearly four a.m.

Bill nodded and turned to the piano player. "Play 'Misty' for us—the Mathis version." He held both my hands in his through all thirty-two bars of the song. As he sang it was as if we were the only two people in the bar and I knew then that I was falling for this guy called "Billy Actor", but who *I* called Bill.

The lights flicked on and off, and Bill chugged the dregs of his drink. "Finish up," he said, "It's closing time."

I sat my half-finished Dewar's and soda on the piano. "I can't finish that," I said, "but I don't want to go home."

Bill pulled my head close to his chest. "Neither do I," he whispered, "there's a beach out front of this place. We could always sit and watch the moon rise."

"It's setting," I said. "It's moonset just about now."

"Moonset...you an astronomer of some kind?" He snickered. "Come on." He pulled me toward the exit. "Let's go down to the beach."

I feigned a Bette Davis flutter and fanned myself with my hands. "Oh, you foolish schemer, you meanin' to take advantage of me?" I said in my worst Southern-Belle accent.

"Only if you'll let me." Bill nudged me past the doorman and out into the warm moist breeze off Lake Ronkonkoma.

It was after four in the morning, and the alcohol and exhaustion were kicking in as we got to the narrow beach that rung the lake.

Bill pulled me down next to him, and I landed in a plop on the hard sand. "You know," I slurred, "I never expected this tonight."

"Neither did I," Bill said as he put his lips to mine.

I pressed my mouth shut tight as his tongue ran across my teeth. I wanted this to be more than just another make-out session that would be forgotten in a week. I pushed him away, sucked in a breath, and said, "Not now...not like this."

The moon cast ghostly shadows between us as it sank into the lake. I pointed up. "Look, the moon's blue."

"Looks more gray than blue to me," Bill said.

I chortled. "You're just not a romantic."

He tried to kiss me again, but I pushed him away. "Do you even know what a romantic is?" I said in my most arrogant teacherly voice.

"Like Byron, Shelly, and those guys?" Bill stuck his tongue out at me. "Yeah, Mr. Know-It-All, they don't call me 'Billy

Actor' for nothing. You know that to act you need to know something about literature, too."

I nestled my head on Bill's chest. "I'm sorry. I underestimated you. I'm a little—"

"Full of yourself?"

I nodded and snuggled closer to the man I'd dubbed "Captain Kirk" just a few hours earlier. "Look, the sun's peeking over the horizon."

Bill glanced at his watch. "Oh, shit. It's five o'clock."

"Well, I'm off until Labor Day so I can sleep tomorrow...but you?"

"I don't have to be in to work until the afternoon. I work the three to eleven shift at Citibank's processing center—didn't I tell you that?"

I shook my head, although I didn't really remember if he'd told me or not. "So, you want to go out again tomorrow night?"

Bill shrugged.

"Like to the Barnyard in Sayville or someplace out in the Hamptons?"

Bill shook his head. "No, I can't do this late-night-after-work thing two nights in a row."

"Well, how about this Saturday?"

Bill gazed toward the rising sun. "Goddammit...I can't!"

I scooched away from him. "Whoa, why so angry?"

"Because it's my twenty-fifth birthday on Saturday, and my sister's throwing me a party."

"So?"

"So...I can't invite you."

"Huh?"

"Paul, it's 1982, but my sister thinks like it's 1952. How am I supposed to explain who and what you are to me to be invited to my quarter-century birthday party?" Bill pulled me into his arms. "Besides, I have to go to work at three in the afternoon, so it's going to be a short affair. But I'm off Sunday and Monday."

I pressed my lips to his. This time I let my mouth take in his sweet breath. As our tongues entwined, it was as if we were one until our long embrace ended. "Let's go," I said and pulled him up from the beach. I brushed the damp sand off his pants as we walked toward the empty parking lot of La Bise.

Bill leaned against his Valiant. "I guess I'll never see you again"

"Rawmaish," I said. I pulled a pencil from the console of my car and scribbled my telephone number on a scrap of paper. "This is my number...well, my parent's number... they have a summer place in the Hamptons; that's where I'm staying while I'm between jobs." Bill took my number and shoved it into his pants pocket. I waited for him to give me his, but he didn't offer and—as gay protocol had it in those days—I didn't dare ask him for it. "If you're not busy Sunday, call me," I said. "We'll do afternoon Tea Dance somewhere."

Bill took me in his arms and kissed me until my knees buckled and I fell backward on the hood of his car. His hand reached for my crotch but, as excited as I was, I pushed him off me. "Not here, not now; don't spoil a perfectly romantic evening"

He let me go. "You know what? When I'm near you, Paul, I feel like that kitten in the tree from *Misty*?"

I felt my face flush. "You know what, Bill? I think I just might chase you up that tree."

Bill grinned. "I'll call you Sunday."

"I'll wait for you."

With the mid-July sun rising over Lake Ronkonkoma, Bill and I shared one more long embrace. When I got into my Gran Prix and started the engine, I rode home on a cloud of ecstasy. The man I met that night filled all the bills of my fantasies.

By the time I got home to West Hampton it was seven in the morning. I jumped in the shower to wash off the sand and sweat from my night out and climbed into bed. I think I fell asleep before my head hit the pillow, but the phone ringing three hours later woke me with a start. I sprung up and grabbed the receiver hoping it was Bill calling to invite me to his birthday party after all.

"May I speak to Mr. Ivey?" a woman's voice asked.

"This is he."

"Hello, Mr. Ivey. This is Mrs. Gruber, Headmaster Bowman's secretary from The Queens Academy."

I cleared my throat trying to sound less groggy. "Yes...yes, how may I help you?"

"Headmaster Bowman would like to set up an interview with you sometime next week."

I swallowed hard trying to hide my excitement at the prospect of getting a real job at a prestigious private school in the city. "Okay, what day and when?"

"How is Tuesday, next week...say around eleven?"

"Okay, eleven it is then. Thank you, Mrs.—"

"Gruber. Headmaster Bowman and Dr. Cohen, our director, will be conducting the interview."

"Should I bring anything? A résumé, or my teaching certificate?"

"No, I have copies of all that. We'll see you on Tuesday, Mr. Ivey."

"Thank you," I said and hung up.

I sat on the edge of my bed and stared out my window overlooking The Great South Bay. "What the fuckity fuck did I step in," I mumbled to myself. "I've fallen in love and got an interview for my fantasy job in less than twenty-four hours." *This is all happening too fast.* I rolled over and pulled the covers over my head hoping that when I woke up it all wouldn't have been just a dream.

I finally dragged myself out of bed around three in the afternoon. Later that evening, I thought about heading out to the Swamp Disco in Wainscott. But instead, I ended up watching summer reruns of *Dallas* and *Falcon Crest*. Deep down, I hoped the phone might ring. By 11:30 I went to bed and slept through Saturday morning, until I heard my mother trudge up the stairs at the far end of the house.

She called to me, and I dragged myself out of bed, dressed, and sat with her in the kitchen while she unpacked groceries for the weekend.

I told her about the job interview on Tuesday. She was happy for me but more concerned that I get outside and ready my father's boat. He had friends coming on Sunday and they wanted to go out fishing, so everything had to be in order. I wasn't invited on my father's fishing expedition, nor did I really want to go, since I was hoping Bill would call to set up a time and place to meet for Tea Dance. But I didn't share that bit of information with my mother. With her Old-World Italian moralities, she would have never understood my anticipation.

By Sunday morning, I sadly resigned myself to the fact that I'd never hear from Bill again. So, I chalked him up as one of those touchy-feely-almost-something encounters that I'd had so many times before. At noon I decided to shower and get ready for Tea Dance. In my room, I pulled together my best summer outfit—tight cutoff shorts and a white, blouson shirt I wore unbuttoned but tied at the waist. After a spritz of Paco Rabanne, I went into the kitchen to tell my mother I was heading out.

"Oh, a fellow called for you while you were in the shower," she said.

My heart skipped a beat. "What?"

"Yeah. It wasn't your friend Pete...I think he said his name was Bob or Bill."

"Bill!" My heart skipped several more beats.

"Yeah, Bill. He wanted me to tell you to meet him at a place called 'Beast...Bisque'? Or something like that."

"Mom, which is it, The Beast or La Bise? One's on Fire Island and the other's on Lake Ronkonkoma."

"I don't think it was the second one you said, there was no 'la' in what I heard."

"Then it's got to be The Beast on the Island. That's where everybody goes for Sunday Tea anyway." I was so excited I pulled my mother into a bear hug. "Don't wait up for me, Mom. I'll see you when I see you." I flew down the stairs, jumped in my car, and raced to catch the next ferry from Sayville to the Grove on Fire Island.

As the boat docked at the Grove, I scanned the board-walk for Bill. I suppose in some deep corner of my mind I was hoping he'd be standing there waiting for me with a bouquet of roses.

Instead, I spotted Walter, my banker friend from Manhattan, standing in ninety-degree heat, in a white long-sleeve shirt, blue jeans, wide-brimmed straw hat, and opaque, black-rimmed sunglasses. I nudged him when I walked up to him. "Hey, Walter, you waiting for somebody?"

"Nah. Just checking out the latest crop of meat coming in," he said in his half-Bugs Bunny-Elmer Fudd voice. "But looks like you'll have to do for now."

I grabbed him by the elbow. "C'mon, I'll buy you a drink at The Beast. I'm supposed to meet somebody there."

The Beast was a monster of a dance club—an open-air space with a huge square bar in the middle, a DJ booth at the far end, and a dance floor that stretched all the way from the boardwalk to the beach. I bellied up to the bar with Walter. "What do you want to drink?" I shouted over Chaka Khan singing about how she was every woman.

"Perrier."

"No alcohol?"

Walter shook his head. "I need to drive back to Manhattan tonight."

I called to the bartender, "Bobby, two small Perrier Waters."

Bobby nodded and pulled two green bottles from the ice bin and handed them to me.

I grabbed Bobby's arm. "Listen, have you seen a guy named Bill?"

He laughed. "There are a hundred Bill's in here now. Bill who?"

"I don't know his last name, but they call him 'Billy Actor.' He looks a little like Captain Kirk from *Star Trek*."

Bobby shrugged. "I think I know who you mean, but I ain't seen him today. He don't come over to the Grove often, and when he does, he usually goes to Off-Off-Broadway, the piano bar by the docks."

Walter elbowed me in the ribs.

I winced. "Ouch, fuckity fuck...what was that for?"

Walter pulled his sunglasses down his nose and fixed his eyes on me. "You meeting Billy Actor?"

"I was hoping to find him here."

"I know the guy. He's a little whore," Walter said in that Bugs Bunny-Elmer Fudd voice of his that got more pronounced the more envious he got. "He works for my bank's processing center in Huntington. His name's William Montague—he lives in Medford."

"What? I grew up in Medford. Listen, Walter, I want to go over to Off-Off-Broadway to see if he's there."

Walter's upper lip curled. "Well, you can go over there and look for him but, like I said, he's a—"

"Yeah, I know, a whore, and you're the Virgin Mary... mostly Mary. A green-eyed Mary at that, you jealous bitch."

Walter gave me the finger then broke into an Elmer Fudd laugh

I pulled him into a bear hug. "You know I love you anyway," I said. "So, if you see Billy Actor walk in, tell him where I am."

Walter kissed me on both cheeks. "See you later, bitch, and good luck."

I ran down the boardwalk and raced up the stairs to the second level of Off-Off-Broadway where the piano player was starting his second set. I scanned the crowd of mostly older men, but Bill wasn't among them. Crestfallen, I gulped down the rest of my warm Perrier water and headed to the downstairs bar for something stronger to drown my sorrows. I flopped onto a stool and looked around the nearly empty space.

The bartender came over. "What'll it be?"

"Dewar's on the rocks—make it a double."

The bartender, a fifty-something-year-old man, poured me a hefty drink and slid it across the bar. He studied me for a minute. "You okay?"

I shook my head and sucked in a deep breath to hold back tears.

"What's the matter, hon? You get jilted?"

"Stood up," I said and let the flood gates open.

The bartender took my hand. "Hey. Hey, now. What happened?"

I took a long swig of my drink, caught my breath, and recounted the whole story of Bill, me, the missed phone call, my mother...

The bartender waved his hand in the air, as much to get me to end my story, as to offer me his advice. "Just call him," he said. He reached under the bar and handed me a Long Island phonebook.

In my mind's eye, a cartoon lightbulb flicked on. *How many William Montagues could there be living in Medford, New York?*

I cracked the thick book opened to the "M's" and scanned through the pages, and there he was, W. Montague, 6 Grassy Lane, Medford. *Oh my God, I grew up six blocks away from there.* I grabbed a pen and a piece of paper off the bar, wrote the number down, and called the bartender over.

"What do I owe you?"

"Did you find the number?"

"I think so, now I need to call. So how much for the drink?"

"It's on me. Now go call him, hon."

I guzzled the rest of my Scotch and headed to the phone booth at the dock. I waited before I put my quarter in the pay slot. *What if I have the wrong Montague, or if his parents answer?* I dialed the number anyway, but the phone rang and rang with no answer. I dialed again, thinking I might have called the wrong number, but the result was the same.

Then it hit me, maybe my mother had mixed up *Beast* and *Bise*, and Bill was in Ronkonkoma. Dockside, the next ferry back to Sayville was getting ready to leave. The gangplank was already up but, against the warnings of the captain and crew, I jumped over the gap between the board-walk and the boat and landed on the stern deck. One of the crewmen came over to me. "You know you just broke the law?" I handed him my ticket and a five dollar bill I had in my pocket. "You never saw me do that," I said.

He shook his head. "Just another day in gay paradise. Grab a seat on the top deck and behave."

I saluted. "Yessir!"

By the time the ferry docked in Sayville, the sun was already setting. I jumped in my car and broke the speed limit on the Expressway until I made it to the Ronkonkoma exit. I drove around the lake in the dark until I spotted the lights of La Bise in the distance.

The parking lot was nearly empty, but I could hear the voices of the male chorus gathered around the piano. When I walked in, there were only five or six patrons in the place, and Bill wasn't among them.

Rusty waved me over to the bar. "Paul, where've you been?"

"At the Grove."

"Oh my God. Bill just left. He was looking for you. He said he told your mother to meet him here. He was none too happy when you didn't show up."

My heart sunk. "Fuckity fuck. Where'd he go?"

Rusty shrugged. "Home I guess, but he might have gone to the Barnyard in Sayville for one last drink. You might want to check there."

I thanked Rusty and ran out to my car. Defying all odds and all speed limits, I raced back to Sayville. I drove around the parking lot of the Barnyard and searched for Bill's blue Valiant. His car was nowhere in sight. It was already past eleven, so rather than go into the bar and waste more time to ask if Bill had been there, I decided to take a chance and find his house in Medford. I knew exactly where Grassy Lane was, and I was pretty sure I could find house number 6. And if I were mistaken, what could be the worst to happen—a night in county jail for trespassing while intoxicated with lust?

The lights in most of the homes in the well-kept neighborhood were dark, but when I pulled up in front of number 6, there was one light glowing in a side room window. I sat in my car for a half hour trying to decide what to do. I couldn't very well go up to the front door, ring the bell, and risk his mother or father coming to the door. But having grown up in that neighborhood, I knew the floorplans of all the houses were pretty much the same, which meant the lit window had to be a spare bedroom—more than likely Bill's room.

I got out of my car, grabbed a fist full of pebbles from the gravel driveway, tossed them at the lit window, and hid behind the shrubbery. I held my breath hoping I had the right house and the right window—it flung open, and Bill's head popped out. "Who's out there?" he shouted.

I kept silent.

"I'm going to call the cops."

"Rawmaish," I hollered from behind a bush.

"What the fuck?"

I stepped out from the shrubbery and walked into the glow of Bill's open window.

He slapped his forehead. "What are you doing here?"

"Looking for you."

"It's after midnight."

"I know. I've been running around Long Island looking for you for the past twelve hours."

"Oh, for Christ's sake." Bill shook his head. "Well, you're here now; you might as well come in."

"What about your parents?"

"They're gone this week. They left to go camping this morning."

A thrill ran through me. *Oh my God, my chance has come.* I walked up to Bill's window and started to climb inside.

He glared at me. "What the hell are you doing?"

"Coming in."

"You drunk?"

I shook my head.

"Come around to the front door, and I'll let you in like a human being...Jesus now."

Bill came to the door in a loose-fitting flannel shirt and a pair of tighty-whities. He pulled me inside. "You *are* crazy."

I nodded. "Remember when I said I'd chase you up a tree? Well, I've been chasing you all day because...because..." I wrapped my arms around him and kissed him hard. "I think I'm in love with you. I've never met a man like you who...who I want to go all the way with."

Bill took two steps back and studied me. "You mean you've never...?

I shook my head.

He picked me up in his arms and carried me into his room. He laid me on his bed. He didn't turn off the light when he slipped off his shirt and underwear. He lay down next to me and ran his fingers through my hair. "I never believed in love at first sight before, but now I do," he whispered and rolled over to turn out the light.

We spent most of the next day in bed. We got up once or twice to use the bathroom and grab a cold snack from the refrigerator. By eight o'clock that Monday night, I told Bill I had to get back to West Hampton to get ready for my interview in Queens the next day. He gave me his work number as I was leaving and told me it was best to call him there anytime between three and eleven. He would rather talk at work without his parents around eavesdropping on his conversations.

During my Tuesday morning drive from West Hampton to The Queens Academy, I began to wonder if the hour-and-a-half commute into Flushing was really worth the $10,000 a year salary that was being offered.

When I arrived at The Academy, I was greeted in the front office by Mrs. Gruber, who led me to an anteroom where I waited for the headmaster and director. I hardly had sat down when two gentlemen came out of a side door and introduced themselves as Dr. Bowman and Dr. Cohen. The two looked alike, both with graying hair and bushy eyebrows. The only way I could distinguish between them was that the headmaster was wearing a bowtie. They led me into an office, and I took a seat at a desk across from them. When they began the interview, their questions seemed only a formality—as if they had already made their decision. Dr.

Cohen explained that my previous work with emotionally disturbed students is what caught their attention on my résumé. Headmaster Bowman dovetailed off the director's comments and said, "Although bright, many of our students at our Academy have some emotional issues that need special attention and, in light of your experience, we're willing to up the salary to $12,000."

My eyes widened.

The headmaster pushed the contract toward me, but Dr. Cohen stopped him before it reached my side of the desk. The director's eyes narrowed. "Let me ask you something, Paul," he said. "You list your address as West Hampton. Are you willing to commute that far every day?"

I put my hand on my chin and looked down. "That crossed my mind. I guess I'll have to find an apartment somewhere in Queens."

Dr. Cohen's eyes lit up. "Well, young man, I might have just the thing for you. My daughter is looking to move into Manhattan, but she wants to sublet her apartment here on Beech Street. It's a one bedroom, but the building is right around the corner. She's asking $350 a month, if you're interested."

I hesitated while I calculated if $650 a month after rent would be enough to cover what it cost to live in the city. "350, plus utilities?" I asked.

Dr. Cohen shook his head. "Utilities are included, and it's furnished."

"Well, that sounds doable."

Headmaster Bowman took the contract to his side of the desk. He whited-out something and wrote over it. He showed it to Dr. Cohen. The director nodded and handed the paper to me. In the salary section, the headmaster had whited-out $12,000 and wrote $12,500 in its place. The two gentlemen smiled as I signed.

Headmaster Bowman shook my hand. "Welcome aboard," he said.

Dr. Cohen stood up. "Welcome aboard indeed, Paul. And I'd like to show you the apartment."

"Now?"

"Sure, I have the keys in my pocket." He came around the desk and put his hand on my shoulder. "I was hoping you'd say yes to the sublet," he whispered. "Let's go see the place, and if you're satisfied, you can sign the sublease, and I'll take you to lunch."

I think I floated from Kessina Boulevard around the corner to the brownstone apartment on Beech Street. During lunch Dr. Cohen and I made small talk about pedagogy and the importance of maintaining high academic standards, but all I could think about was getting home and calling Bill to tell him the amazing news.

The hour-and-a-half drive back to West Hampton took four in rush-hour traffic. When I got home, I didn't even take time to use the bathroom before I called Bill. He picked up his extension on the first ring. "William Montague, Citibank processing center, how may I help you?"

"Jesus, you're sexy on the phone."

Bill chuckled. "Oh, rawmaish. What're you up to?"

"I got good news—I got the job."

"Wow!"

"Yeah, and..." I took a deep breath. "And I want you to celebrate with me this weekend."

"Where, when, and how?"

"Sunday, in Wainscott, at La Luna Nuda restaurant," I said.

Bill laughed. "Funny name for a restaurant, but I'm in...except four days is an awful long time to wait...to... you know..."

"It'll make it all that much more thrilling when we see each other again." I thought about telling Bill about the apartment, but I figured that could wait until we had dinner.

Just then, his other extension rang. "I gotta go, Paul, but call me tomorrow, and every day after that."

When I hung up, I leaned back in my chair and stared up at the ceiling. *Could Bill really be the man I've been looking for all my life?*

To save Bill the hassle of trying to find his way to my parent's house in West Hampton, I decided to pick him up in Medford, then we'd drive out east to La Luna Nuda, a cozy Northern Italian restaurant in Wainscott.

We didn't talk much during the drive. I complained about the summer traffic and the day trippers from the city who hadn't a clue where they were going, let alone how to drive. Bill just hummed along with the tunes on the radio; from time to time he'd break out in song. His voice had the timbre of a young Tony Bennett and the vibrato of Johnny Mathis. It didn't matter what he sang, he made me swoon with every note.

The parking lot of La Luna Nuda was filling up when we got there. I had to park along the highway to avoid getting boxed in—a common occurrence in small, Hampton eateries during tourist season.

When we sat down at the table I'd reserved, we began to look over the menu. Then I recalled the restaurant's menu was only in Italian and the wait staff spoke little English. Not a problem for me since Italian was my first language, but Bill was lost.

"Well, what do you like to eat?" I asked.

"Veal."

"Okay, *vitello.* How do you want it? They've got *alla parmigiana, francese, scapariello, marsala.*"

He smiled. "It all sounds delicious when you say it, but I have no idea what all that means."

I went through the list and explained the preparations of the various veal dishes. He finally settled on a sure thing—*vitello alla parmigiana.*

I called the waiter over and put in our food order along with a bottle of Amarone Ripasso—a wine I adored but really couldn't afford. When the sommelier came to the table and started his "show" of uncorking the wine with a flourish and a swirl, I stopped him and said, *"Non pensare che ti pagherò piu per il show, solo versa il vino."*

The sommelier let out a huff and marched off.

Bill laughed, "What did you tell him?"

"I told him, 'Don't think I'm going to pay you more for the show, just pour the wine.'"

"Oh my God, you're harsh."

"It's not harsh. I'm not paying extra for rawmaish."

We laughed so hard we almost spilled our wine. We clinked glasses and toasted to my newfound job and apartment.

"And speaking of apartments..." I took another sip of wine, put down my glass, and reached into my pocket. I pulled out a small, velvet pouch and handed it to Bill.

He furrowed his brow. "What's this?"

"Well, open it."

He pried open the pouch and shook out what was inside. "A key?"

"To my apartment in Queens."

"For me?"

I nodded. "Or us...if you want to come live with me."

Bill put his hand on his chin. "Paul, we've known each other for two weeks."

"And?"

"And you're asking me to live with you?"

"If you want to."

Tears welled in Bill's eyes. He reached across the table for my hand and squeezed it in his. "I want to be with you every minute of the day...nobody has ever knocked me so head over heels like you."

I poured us each another glass of Amarone. "Do you say yes?"

"I do."

Epilogue

Bill and I had been monogamous partners for twenty-nine years when we were legally married in 2011. During our life together, we shared the kind of relationship that gay and straight couples envied. But God's plan was bigger than ours. In 2016—two days after my sixtieth birthday—Bill died of a sudden, massive heart attack at the age of sixty-two. The night we went out to celebrate my milestone birthday, his wish for me was to keep writing and publish the novel I was working on at that time.

I dedicate this story and every word I write to him.

Chatroom Love

by Marie Montgomery

Hey, want to chat?

Back in the early days of the internet, when I said, "We met online," the look of horror on the faces of my friends and family was palpable.

One did not simply meet the love of their life online in the 90s. Yeah, you met shady catfishes online in 1998, but not the man you wanted to spend the rest of your life with. But, always interested in doing things which made my parents rush to fearful conclusions, I bucked that trend and met my now-husband of seventeen years in a chatroom using the screen name Bubbles. God knows what nineteen-year-old me was thinking.

The day we met I was home from college for the summer, bored out of my mind and exploring this new thing called the Internet from my childhood bedroom. I wasn't really looking for something romantic, was just looking to talk with people virtually. I jumped into a Florida political chat room, being a political science minor at the time, and started talking with the group. James' profile stood out. His screen name was "Mad Cavalier" ... I was intrigued and started chatting with him directly, almost like you would these days in a DM. If I recall correctly, my intro was "Hey, I like your profile." Smooth.

Back in those days your profile consisted of an image of some sort, not a photo, and a descriptive sentence. But beyond that, you had no idea who you were talking with. The person on the other end of the computer was an unknown in many ways. For some reason, no rational thought struck me at that point and I dove right into having personal conversations with a stranger. We first started with some light small talk. Talked about where we lived, our lives as students and our interests. After the first conversation all I knew was that he had an interest in politics and history, lived in Florida, and was witty. I was not online looking for love. I just wanted to make a connection and explore. Yet, he drew me in.

What do you look like?

We really hit it off in our chats and over the next few weeks we made dates to talk in a private chat room. Our small talk quickly escalated to flirting with conversations that explored what we could have beyond the computer screen.

MadCavalier: So, tell me, do you have a boyfriend?

Bubbles: No. I did about a year ago, but no one has caught my interest since then.

MadCavalier: Why? What are you looking for?

Bubbles: Well, first, someone taller than me ;-) ... I'm 5'9" and my last date ended horribly because he couldn't get over the fact that I was taller than him.

MadCavalier: Good to know. I'm 6'2" :-)

Bubbles: Well, that's promising. :)(:

MadCavalier: Did you just send me a kiss?

Bubble: Maybe ;-)

The conversations grew from there and we finally agreed to share our phone numbers with each other, which, of course, were land-line phone numbers.

Our first phone call was sweet but awkward and it quickly became evident that he was much more outgoing than I was. James led the conversation as he asked me question after question, and we talked in more detail about our lives. He lived in a college town four hours away from me, but we continued to talk like this on the phone for weeks. We scheduled times around our classes and jobs, finding hours late at night and very early in the morning to talk. We continued to learn about each other and extend our online connection into the real world.

Then about one month into our chat relationship, we decided it was time to mail each other a picture. *I was self conscious about mailing a picture – at the time I did not have many pictures of just me. There were no cell phone cameras or selfies in 1998, so photos involved film and printing ... a lot of effort. And, at this point, I had not told anyone about James and our conversations, so I couldn't raise anyone's suspicions by asking help in taking a special picture of me.* I was always a one-date girl, never willing to go past the second date if I wasn't into a guy. And I NEVER EVER introduced my dates to my parents. That was a no go in all situations because I couldn't even consider putting a guy through the parent moment if I was pretty sure we were not going anywhere. *So, I went looking through pictures from the past year to find one where I looked good and cute.*

He also rummaged through our printed photos and found one to share. And coincidentally, we ended up mailing each other photos with our families. His featured a young man with short blonde hair standing amongst a group of older women, his gaggle of six aunts. Mine pictured me with my younger sister and grandmother. I loved getting his picture – he was tall and cute with a wide smile that portrayed a sincere and happy person.

Our pictures were not staged, there were no filters, and I am not even sure if I had makeup on in mine. So, while not amazing pictures by any means, they were honest depictions of who we were. And, to each other's surprise, it brought our virtual relationship closer. I knew then that I needed to meet him in real life. *But how was that going to happen? Was it a good idea?* Because, I knew, if we did not have the same chemistry in person that we had online this sweet relationship would come to an end, and I wasn't ready to give up my talks with James.

"You've Got Mail"

About a week or two later on my twentieth birthday, I wasn't anticipating much. When my mom knocked on my door with a package in hand a vase with two roses—one red and one white—my heart quickened. I had never received a gift at home from a boy.

So, upon handing my mystery package and roses, my mother suspiciously raised her eyebrows and smirked as to say, *I know something is going on here, but I won't ask just yet.*

Shutting the door firmly as she turned and walked away, I rushed to my daybed to open the package after setting the roses, one white and one red, on my dresser.

Inside were three things. A letter wishing me a happy birthday, a Sarah McLachlan CD (one of my favorite musicians of the time), and a bag of jellybeans, his favorite treat.

The letter wished me a happy birthday in simple and well composed words and explained that the white rose was for friendship, the red rose for romantic love. In this moment James showed me that he was more than the man I was talking to online – he was someone I could possibly, maybe, build a relationship with offline in the real world. He had found a way into my heart. And we hadn't even met in person yet.

Can we meet?

In the weeks that followed, I prepared to go back for my junior year of college and we continued to talk on the phone. But we had yet to meet. We both wanted to, but wondered if what we had begun to feel for each other would be there in real life. It is easy to connect online where you are not in each other's physical presence. *Would the spark we felt when talking be there when we're face to face? Would it be easy or awkward?* We really had no idea and the only way to figure out was to meet, talk and look in each other's eyes to see if there was anything there.

Eventually he decided to come to Orlando to visit his mother and asked if we could meet up. So, we picked a place near his mom's south of the city and I hopped in my little Honda Civic and headed out to meet the "guy I met online." Meeting someone you found online was like walking into a blind date, so I made sure my parents and a few friends knew where I was going. I was so nervous, but also excited. I've always been an introvert and talking in person with a boy I liked was so hard on me, but we'd gone past being acquaintances so there was some comfort in that he really knew me well before we met face-to-face. I was hoping he'd see past my awkward nature to the girl he knew. Fingers and toes were crossed.

In the lead up to our date, I'd spent days trolling the local mall looking for the right dress and sandals to wear, and that day I painstakingly blew out my long, strawberry blonde hair and applied just the right amount of makeup to impress, but not go overboard.

That night I finally got in my car and hit the expressway to meet him about forty-five minutes away from my parent's house. I had given myself one hour to get there. But as soon as I merged onto the interstate, I encountered a major back-up due to a traffic accident. At that time, I did not have a cell phone, but he did, and I had the number.

So ... I got off at an exit about fifteen miles away and found a gas station with a pay phone and dialed him. I knew I would be incredibly late and, in no way, wanted him to think I had stood him up. I dropped my quarters in the pay phone, dialed and ... "Ring ... ring ... ring ...ring." He did not answer. So, I left what I am sure was a panicked and rambling voice mail, ran back to my car, and got back on the interstate. I did my best daredevil driving, weaving through the traffic the best I could and finally arrived at our date location more than thirty minutes late. I wasn't even sure if he would still be there.

I parked in a panic, and jogged to our pre-set meeting location, looking around frantically to find him. Within seconds I spotted him as his eyes met mine, lighting up as I gave him a strained smile. He stood there wearing a white shirt with a collar and jeans that, to be honest, were a little too tight, but fit him perfectly. There was kindness in his face as I approached. "James?" I said. "Marie?" was his simple response before pulling me into a tight bear hug, giving me instant calm before my embarrassment at being late could sink in. Seeing him for the first time in real life felt like a relief – like my heart and chest had been held tight for days and were finally able to relax.

I was mortified about being late, but after sharing so much of myself over the phone and internet in the months prior, it felt weird talking in person. Ever the gentleman, he persisted through my shyness. He got me to open up in person, talk, laugh, and eventually kiss.

HOW I MET MY OTHER

Our date was at a local entertainment complex used mainly by tourists, so there were tons of things for us to do as we walked and got to know each other. We settled on one of the better restaurants and enjoyed dinner together, then walked and talked, easily holding hands as we went. Eventually the crowds thinned as it inched toward midnight and we settled on a bench in a more secluded area of the complex. As I cuddled up into his warmth on that bench, I knew it was time for a kiss. And, wow, did we kiss. It started as a sweet peck with his hands in mine. Then it escalated as we explored each other with our mouths and hands, as if the tension that had built over the past weeks flirting over the phone simply exploded. We lost all sense of time. So much so, that a security guard had to kick us out at the end of the night like two crazy teenagers.

It was an amazing night and started us on our path together.

Thinking back now, that first night we met in person was a new chapter in my life. Before that I had goals and dreams. But I had also gone through the previous years without much of a purpose. I did all the college stuff – classes, internships, sorority, parties, etc. – but there was no real focus or purpose beyond those moments. His presence in my life helped me focus on life beyond school, beyond academic achievement and beyond ticking the boxes of life.

Over the next few weeks, he stayed in Orlando, and we truly began to build a bond. The time finally came when school was starting up again and he needed to head back to Tallahassee and I needed to move back on campus. It was a tense moment and felt like our time was coming to an abrupt end. The real world and its responsibilities were pulling us away from each other.

I do not remember much about this time except for the moment right before we said goodbye. He had come over to spend time with me and have lunch with my family before his four-hour drive home. He politely said goodbye to my parents and sister, and we walked hand in hand out to my parent's suburban driveway. We stood hugging as he leaned up against his car when I suddenly blurted out, *"What are we?"* He let out a small laugh which I am sure was followed by one of my signature scowls and simply said "I think it's obvious what we are. You are my girlfriend and I am, hopefully, your boyfriend." My happiness, and relief, was instant, as I snuggled into his hug with a soft smile on my face saying "Yes, you are my boyfriend."

I did not know it at the time, but the ease we had in deciding that we were officially a couple foreshadowed so many life decisions that we had ahead of us. We were in sync with each other. We knew what we wanted.

Time ...

Over the next five years we both hit many milestones in our lives. He moved to Orlando to be with me and settled into school and a job. I graduated college and started working in my degree field of public relations, and we began slowly building a life together.

The subject of marriage came up all the time – but I was firm: he needed to finish college before we could get married.

While he is older than me, he started school a few years behind me after a stint in the Navy and working in politics. I knew that finishing the degree milestone was important to his future. We also never moved in with each other. That was definitely a break with the norm those days, but for some reason it felt better to be more traditional. It was partially because we knew our cathedral church required couples who were married there to be living apart prior to the wedding, but I think it was also because our meeting in such a different way for the time, led us to be more traditional in other ways. We were both pretty normal people. The fact we met online always seemed to stun those who got to know us because we acted like college sweethearts.

It was during these five years that the inevitability of us eventually being married settled in. Everyone around us simply stopped asking when we would be engaged because we all knew it would happen someday. I remember being at ease about the fact, but I allegedly asked all the time when it would happen (I do not remember nagging, but I did apparently). Someday was always the answer, but we were in our twenties and weren't in a rush. We traveled. We went out and enjoyed the world and settled into a couple routine that was easy.

The preamble ...

It was about a year after he graduated college, when I was working full time while living at home with my parents to save money, that marriage started to be more important to our conversations and plans. We continued attending church together, spending every non-working moment together and talked about what we wanted in a wedding and life together. I anticipated a proposal around every major event and holiday, but still, he didn't ask. *Come on! Just ask me already!*

Apparently about six months prior to proposing, he took my dad out to dinner to ask for my hand. My dad happily obliged. But the formality of "asking for my hand" was just another example of how we often merged more traditional moments with new ideas.

A very wise, calm and loving man, my dad encouraged James and didn't push him. But he did repeat what my grandfather had told him when he asked to marry my mom: "Put your toes where your heels are and run, son!" It was a joke, but is often repeated in our family when anyone attempts to get close to a Montgomery woman.

Will you be my wife?

He finally asked me to marry him on the single most busy day of the year in my family – Christmas Eve.

Christmas Eve in my family is a giant monster that must be fed with lots of activity. There is food to prep for the next several over-the-top meals, gifts to wrap, church to get to and always some last-minute thing to do to ensure that

Christmas is absolutely perfect. My two sisters, mom, dad and I are something of a Martha Stewart family in all honesty and making holidays perfect is something that we have always done. Mom was a home ec teacher prior to having children, and she taught us how to cook, decorate and entertain from the moment we were old enough to help out in the kitchen and around the house.

My job that day was to bake the overnight cinnamon rolls for Christmas morning from scratch. I wore workout shorts, an old t-shirt, no makeup and most likely, my glasses and no bra all while being covered in flour and sugar. Clearly, I was dressed for one of the most important days of my life.

Just as I was finishing up my baking job, he strolled into the house saying "Come on, we're going for a picnic." My reaction was, "Really? Now! Come on, honey. There is so much to do, I cannot go for a picnic in the middle of Christmas Eve."

But somehow, he convinced me that a picnic was due and since we live in Florida, it was pretty warm outside and, in all honesty, seemed like a nice break in the day that I really needed. So, I jumped in the car with him.

He drove through town and meandered through the beautiful streets of Winter Park, Florida—a neighboring community and home to some of the most beautiful homes, lakes, and streets in the state. The car stopped at Kraft Azalea Park, an absolutely stunning park full of giant cypress and oak trees, and large grass areas overlooking a majestic lake.

We jumped out and grabbed all the stuff he had prepared—a large blanket, champagne, strawberries and cream, and all my favorite snacks. It was at this point that I knew something was up. I was also about to jump out of my skin with emotion. I loved my James, but being the planner was generally my job, so I think I was more nervous for him than anything. I usually buy and pack all the stuff and make sure we are supplied, while he serves as the navigator for most of our outings.

We found a wide, grassy spot under a large canopy of Spanish moss-covered oaks overlooking the lake. After setting up the picnic, we settled in as I tried to take over setting up the picnic out of habit. I pulled out the food he had brought – strawberries, whipped cream, chocolate, and champagne. He calmly took the champagne from me, opening it and saying, "Let me do this. Sit back and relax."

He was so nervous. Now, James does not get nervous. He can speak to a room of hundreds of people without issue. He can command attention in any conversation, get to know someone's life story in moments, and is never afraid to share what he is thinking. But at this point, he was clearly nervous as he wouldn't look me in the eye and stumbled to find his words. I pretty much knew what was coming next. *I hoped.*

I remember he started his proposal while I was kneeling on the blanket. He stood, wiped his brow and took a poem he had wrote out of his pocket. Oh God how do I wish I still had the poem. We have both searched and searched for it without success. But I remember the sentiment.

He said, with tears in his eyes, "You know, I prayed my partner for life to come along just months before I met you? You complete me and I want to make a life together."

When he ended his poem and discreetly wiped moisture from his eyes, he knelt down to meet me where I sat crying joyful tears and asked me to be his wife with a beautiful ring showcasing my favorite gemstone, my birthstone the ruby, at the center.

I gave an enthusiastic "yes" as he slipped on the ring. We hugged and kissed as he let out a major sigh of relief. He never had any reason to worry about my answer, but the buildup to this moment had been intense and coming over the last five years.

After spending some more time alone enjoying each other and our engagement picnic, my now fiancé and I returned home where we shared the news with our waiting family. Not one of them knew what was happening. He had planned everything on his own and kept the secret for weeks.

Now one would expect hugs of congratulations when announcing they are engaged. We did receive some of that and tears from my parents, but it was mostly a lot of "*It's about time!*" moments. There were many phone calls with family and friends around the country to announce our news with all sharing in our joy, while immediately asking when we were making it official.

Over the next few weeks, we simply enjoyed the holidays and being engaged before the wedding planning monster took over.

I was at peace and having this overwhelming sense of joy that we were heading down the right path to building our life and family as a loving team. Thinking back all these years later, I am still overcome with a feeling of soft, centering joy. I had found my soul mate in an online chat room. We had built a relationship over years, changed our life paths for each other and now, here we were, ready to commit to each other for the rest of our existence in this life. I was truly in a state of soft, anticipatory happiness.

Epilogue – A Wedding in a Year of Hurricanes

In November 2004, I finally walked down the aisle wearing a champagne beaded wedding gown in a grand cathedral in downtown Orlando. Having our faith at the center of our wedding was key for us. And, wow, did we need it to get through the planning months.

All for our wedding was on track until August 2004 when Central Florida was struck by not one, but three hurricanes—Charley, Frances, and Jeanne. These three horses of the hurricane apocalypse were not playing around and managed to cause major damage throughout the state. Charley was by far the most destructive, a category four hurricane that quickly tore a path from southwest Florida on up through Orlando. It took homes, trees, and thousands of power lines down. Not only did Charley wreak havoc on my parents' neighborhood, it entirely destroyed our planned honeymoon location in Captiva Island and ensured we had to stop planning our wedding details for at least four to six weeks while everyone pulled their lives back together.

So, as a planner by nature, those few months were absolutely frustrating for me. I had to pause planning some elements, struggle with the budget, find a whole new honeymoon location, and work to ensure all of our vendors were still able to provide what we needed for our wedding a few months later.

In the end it all worked out, but it was a fire drill that, in a way, prepared us for married life to come. After seventeen years married, I can tell you it is darn hard. Your life changes, arguments ensue, there are times of emotional drought, and kids bring joy, challenges and fear into the relationship that you are by no means prepared for. But it is all worth it in ways you could never imagine.

My husband is my rock. He knows all my secrets, weaknesses, fears, and dreams. He has seen me at my worst, my best, and my most dark times, but we continue to find joy, love, and passion together. Our journey is not unlike others, but is ours in unique ways that no other couple in history will ever have.

Who would have known that a chance meeting in an online chat room in 1998 would have produced the love and story we have together?

It did and I am forever and immensely grateful for the power of the internet and divinely inspired fate of our meeting.

Another Chance at Love

Extraordinary Engagement

by E.M. Hector

The practical voice inside my head said, *Stop, he's younger than you.* The curious voice quipped, *But he is single and handsome, and he seems to like kids.* The cautious voice argued, *What have you got to offer?* That was the kind of mental banter that often rattled back and forth in my mind. It popped up without warning whenever I assessed the possibility of building an intimate personal relationship after being divorced five years earlier.

You could say that we met accidentally through Ruth, a mutual friend. We all lived in the same rent-subsidized apartment complex, positioned around a central courtyard. Each unremarkable block building consisted of ten apartments, five up and five down. He and I lived in different buildings, both upstairs. He was North. I was East. In the beginning, I believed we lived in different universes. Sharing an imaginary compass quadrant was close enough for me. I had become an expert at keeping personal relationships at arm's length.

On pleasant afternoons between school and work, and on weekends, Julio and his roommates tossed the football or frisbee around in the courtyard with the younger kids in the complex. Ruth and I sat on the top of the open outdoor stairwell and enjoyed the view of *all* the boys playing together.

She plopped down next to me on the top step after work one day, slipped the sandals off her sunburned feet, and announced, "I'm quitting work and going to apply to nursing school full-time." Her ambition inspired me. To be brave enough to leave her paying job, take on school debt, continue to manage three young kids and all of their associated activities, while thinking positive about a better future, was motivating. All I could say was "WOW!".

In the next breath, together we shouted, "Gregory, Ronnie, Mikey, David! You boys need to come inside now." Ruth and I took turns calling our kids in from the courtyard just to see those guys pause and look in our direction. Their athletic bodies in cut-off tee-shirts and comfortable shorts exposed more than sun-drenched muscles. Oh, believe me, Ruth was the instigator, no doubt about it.

To understand my story, keep in mind all the definitions and synonyms of the word engagement. To begin, I wouldn't exactly describe it as a romantic engagement. A serious single mom does not go gaga after a man younger than herself, let alone a college man.

During the day, he attended classes at the university, working towards his second college degree. He went to work after school, and then went out dancing with friends in the evening. That was until he broke his foot playing an outdoor game of basketball in off-court shoes.

He limped into Ruth's house in pain and asked, "Got any ice? I think I need some ice…I may have broken my foot." He showed her his rapidly swelling and bruised ankle. In a mad rush to find some ice for the swelling, our mutual friend sent her nine-year-old daughter out to see if anyone had ice. Her daughter knocked on several apartment doors without success and then she knocked on mine.

Mandy excitedly said, "I need ice. Mom thinks Julio broke his ankle."

My small freezer held two icetrays. I popped the cubes out of the trays, put them into a plastic bag, handed them to her, and sent her on her way. Mission completed. At the time, I wasn't quite sure which one of those college guys belonged to that name.

Ruth's boys and my boys were close in age, and when they got together outdoors, they were often wild. To wind down after a long day we singles would get together after dinner at Ruth's apartment for some grown-up time, and our children would find something relatively quiet to do together in their room.

The college guy, whom I soon learned was Julio, couldn't go dancing for a while with a cast on his leg, but he still went to work. He would hobble over after work, and we would all share a cup of instant coffee. Back then, a needed cup of coffee, instant or otherwise, was pretty special for us single moms. Julio taught us how to make it taste better with a lot of milk, a pinch of salt, and a dash of cinnamon. Heated to just the right temperature, we shared a cup of that pleasantly aromatic concoction.

Ruth and I would browse through the latest issue of Cosmopolitan magazine and goad him into giving us his young male perspective on the monthly pop fad surveys. It was interesting to hear his point of view on everything from trendy fashions and entertainment to the latest fragrance sample inserted into each issue.

On weekend get-togethers at Ruth's, later into the night, the exhausted kids finally fell asleep. When it was time to go, I found myself nudging my older son saying, "Come on, sleepyhead," as I struggled to carry the younger one up the stairs, home to bed. Julio was there to help. The next morning, I would hear Julio knocking on our door, carrying his own bowl of Special K, ready to join us for breakfast. Endearing. Charming. I was almost ready to melt into his protective arms.

After the ice caper, Julio endeared himself to us. Us, all of us, not just romantically for me, but genuine concern and a positive male presence for my boys. I still don't understand what drew that college guy to us. With two boys under nine years old, besides the responsibilities of motherhood, I was carrying a lot of emotional baggage and didn't consider myself attractive to anyone.

Talk about engagement. Yes, I was engaged—in working, child-rearing, managing a household, all those things now described as adulting. Soon, I found myself otherwise engaged, in adult conversation, in reawakened feelings of being loved, of feeling hopeful instead of hopeless. My walls of resistance were crumbling, and I had not even noticed.

With two young kids around, stealing a little time for romance was a challenge. I was cautious about outwardly showing affection to someone who might not be in it for the long haul. Gentle knocks on my apartment door after his late shift at work, and after kids had gone to bed, allowed us adult alone time. He helped me love myself. It was hard to keep our hands off each other. We both wanted the same thing.

Meanwhile, I kept my single life routine. I sent the kids to school. I went to work. At my house, we did homework and hustled to sports practice several afternoons on week-days. We went to pint-sized soccer games and church on weekend mornings. Mostly, my single life was controlled chaos. I didn't think I had room for anyone else. I felt poor, not only poor in spirit but financially strapped. I didn't even have a home phone. The local on-site payphone was my only instant connection to grandparents and family members. As the proud owner of a much older model used car, some days it turned out that I didn't have dependable transportation either. On those days I had to walk my youngest to daycare and myself to work. He often worked on my car when it conked out. I was beginning to believe I had not only found an altruistic partner, but one who was willing to prove his love for me.

Thinking of my inspirational friend Ruth, I reminded myself that I *did* have a full-time job and soon decided it was time to move up and out of that rent-subsidized apartment. I was determined to improve our lives.

Over the next three years, I moved four times to places I could afford on my meager income. Each time Julio helped me move, patiently loading and unloading my house-hold goods. I must have exhausted the man. Each time I announced that I had found another place to live, I'm fairly sure he was thinking, not again as his eyeballs rolled to the back of his head. Although we spent a lot of time together, we never lived together.

It was a matter of circumstance and time before he too moved out of the complex and bought his own home. His house was plenty big for all of us. It was near the boys' schools. I think he secretly hoped that the boys and I would move in with him and he would never have to load or unload our stuff again. He never asked and I never assumed that is what he wanted. I was also stubborn, and independent. I didn't want to burden him with my baggage.

Following his home purchase, I found a realtor to work with me and informed him, "The boys and I are finally looking for a house so we can stop moving around so much." Julio may have thought me crazy, or he may have signed with relief. He never let on one way or another.

One year later, I bought my own home. He helped me move once again. That was my fifth move in probably as many years. To tell the truth, I lost track of how many times I moved but I knew it was time to stop. The boys needed some stability. I looked at their school pictures and realized that they had been in too many schools in their young lives. He was genuinely happy that I finally believed in myself enough to take the step towards homeownership. Qualifying for financing was a huge accomplishment for me. My divorced damaged psyche was recovering. I was now engaged to a mortgage for the foreseeable future.

About that time, we often exercised another definition of engagement. We shared cooking meals and kitchen clean-up, laundry day, church on Sunday, visits with friends, fetch with the dog, and sports and homework with the boys. He always seemed more thoughtful, mature, and sincere than other men I had met. Without any input from me, he gave up going out dancing for a more domestic lifestyle.

As the calendar flipped over each year, there were also times we engaged in battle when opinions clashed on whether to continue our relationship or not. Sometimes I felt like he was sending me mixed messages. He was dedicated to our personal relationship but apprehensive at the same time. I was beginning to wonder whether all the time we spent together was likely to go any further.

"It's been five years and we have never met your family," I complained.

I wondered whether he was hiding something, or whether we were not worthy to meet them. His family lived six hours away in south Florida. He may argue this point, but he was a Cuban male and maybe there was pressure to find a more suitable companion, someone other than a slightly older, divorced woman with two children. Or maybe even one that was fluent in Spanish, which I was not. I found out the right time had just not presented itself.

The early seventeenth-century definition of the word engagement is of French origin, meaning to pledge, in general out of legal obligation or moral sense. We had become close enough to pledge a moral obligation. After all, we were living in modern times, and many families blended without the benefit of a legal commitment. We had no legal obligation to each other and maybe being conservative, that is what riled me after so long. Maybe at the five-year mark that is what I was looking for, but I had no right to demand more than he was willing to offer. The legal part had to wait until *he* was ready.

He would eventually agree that our blending become legal. "I've got to be comfortable enough that I can support a family before I make a lifetime commitment," he said. For me, that was proof enough that he was serious about our

95

future. He finished his school term and soon found a good job in our community allowing us to take our relationship one step further.

It wasn't the Wedding March, but the song lyrics of "Rings" by Lobo (1974 album Just a Singer) that kept playing in my head. We picked out rings, traditionally a symbol of love, a circle that has no beginning and no end. I picked out his, a gold band, with bas-relief vertical bars all around, and two vertical rows each inset with three small diamonds. My own was a two-part swirl of gold embracing three small diamonds. The ring with the three small diamonds was the engagement ring. The three diamonds for me stood for the family of three that my boys and I had been for so long.

Maybe the symbolism of diamonds, the hardest stone known, served as a reminder of how hard it is to maintain a good relationship and how difficult it is when you add hard-headed family members to the mix. Diamonds are also referred to as the stone of invincibility. Though symbolic, I needed this small reassurance that we were committed to each other. I wore that ring proudly.

I eagerly looked forward to the next phase, a solid gold band with a little swirl to envelop us, gather us in and tie us safely together. It was the wedding band.

Through the years, before he put that ring on my finger, there were plenty of snickers from family and friends about me and Julio down by the schoolyard. Julio was not a common name in my life circle, and their only reference to anything Julio was a 1972 catchy upbeat song titled "Me and Julio Down By The Schoolyard" by Paul Simon. Coincidentally, every time his name was mentioned, that line from that tune echoed throughout the room.

My mother was thrilled that I found someone who treated me well, and accepted, cared, and took shared responsibility for my children. Her vision for our future engagement was to have another full-fledged wedding, to invite family members and friends. It had been sixteen years since we had done that with my first marriage, and that hadn't ended so well. I was not fully engaged in her line of thinking. I told her "no big to-do" more than once.

Eight years after Julio's university graduation, his first college degree proved worthwhile and made him the perfect candidate for a new job. In January 1991, he was offered employment 120 miles away from where we both lived. The company agreed to put him in corporate housing for six months. The boys and I continued to live in our house in our town while he rented his house out. It was during that time, after knowing each other for six years, sharing good times, and tough times, experiencing highs and lows, that we both came to the same conclusion.

I was relieved when he, at last, said, "We can make this work. Let's do this!"

Yes, you heard that right. After six years of engagement, in one form, or another, we decided to make it legal. Granted, it is not your textbook bridal engagement story.

My college man and I laughed about our slight age difference, picked a date on the calendar, took care of the necessary paperwork required by the state, and then had an unexpected roadblock thrown our way.

We were both young enough and planned to have a child together. It was a sad day when I awoke from exploratory surgery, three weeks prior to our chosen date, to find out that would never happen. We were both shocked and devastated by the results of my surgery. We put our intended marriage on hold, did some deep thinking, soul searching, and reassessed our future together. It was selfish for me to push through with this relationship if not having a child together was something we would both regret in the years to come.

Our future was on pause.

Two months after my surgery, having gained personal time off through his new job, on a hot, muggy, random August Monday, in the middle of the afternoon, we went down to the county courthouse and got married. My two sons and two of our best friends were witnesses. Everything about that day was low-key. We made no fuss about anything.

At the appointed time, our official witnesses came over from where they worked, one dressed in his A/C company uniform. He intended to return to work that afternoon. The other official witness, our mutual friend Ruth who started it all, came in her work clothes. When the courthouse notary recited the rather traditional wedding vows and asked us to pledge in the presence of our witnesses, "To take each other to be lawfully wed, to have and to hold from this day forward, for better, for worse, for richer, for poorer, in sickness and in health, to love and to cherish, till death do us part." We both looked at each other tenderly and said, "I do."

After the simple ceremony, my youngest son proclaimed, "Now I get to change my name too!"

Both sons signed the marriage certificate, certifying this engagement that has lasted thirty years.

We called my parents afterward and told them to meet us at the local Chinese restaurant for lunch to celebrate. If my mom was disappointed at not having a formal wedding or a big to-do, she never mentioned it. "Congratulations!" was the word of the day. There were handshakes, hugs, and happiness all around. Julio had finally become a household word.

For an entire year, Julio commuted back and forth on the weekend, while we sought a place to live together in the same county as his new job. We had quite a conundrum to sort out and questioned how we would ever qualify for another mortgage because between us we owned three pieces of real estate. Maybe it was divine intervention, maybe it was fate, maybe the universe was in our favor, but by some stroke of luck, by that November after we were married, we found a home that was offered for sale by the owner. The owner was willing to take a chance on us and finance the mortgage. It was near our workplaces and schools and suited us perfectly. We signed off on our new home before Thanksgiving, grateful to be able to make another move towards our complete relationship.

We progressed to a long-term engagement in a fully combined household on December 21, 1991. This was the one move Julio did not have to personally help pack and load. His employer-contracted moving company packed up all of my household goods from 120 miles north a few days earlier and pulled their truck into our new driveway on that date and unloaded everything. We finally advanced to living together, engaged in what families do. Christmas that year was a celebration of commitment and togetherness.

Thirty years later he proudly announces, "Thank goodness our final engagement has cut down on moving household goods around the state. Did you know, we have been in the same house for the last twelve years, and before that eighteen years?"

"Still endearing and still charming after all this time," I say out loud. "C'mon, only two moves in thirty years...you have to agree, it is a marked improvement, considering my history."

Call it what you will. We were actively engaged. In the six years before it was official, we experienced engagement in all forms, on all levels: arrangements, meetings, visits, conflict, and commitment. An extraordinary engagement indeed.

I embrace the man I love, in the tightest bear hug ever. Together we pray to be engaged for the next thirty years.

Easy

by Dan Carroll

I had given up on the idea that God made a life mate for me. I resigned that I was going to be the crazy dog man of Englewood. I had zero expectations, but Jennifer had an evil plan, and the trap was set.

We met on an online Christian dating site. What first captivated me was her big blue eyes. I couldn't stop looking at her pictures. We texted and then talked. We seemed to hit it off, but could she be real?

I pulled my car into the parking lot at six fifty-five, for a seven o'clock first-date conversation over ice cream. Why was I here? I raised my boys and dated all the wrong women for over twenty years. Was I looking for someone who didn't exist? All I wanted was someone to complement my life. Someone to do things with, someone to grow old with besides my dogs.

Fate took over when I parked my car next to an SUV with an attractive woman leaning against the hood. When I speed-dialed Jennifer, I saw the woman leaning on the car answering her phone.

When I saw Jennifer, I thought, *Yeah, I can date her for a while.* There she was, a stunningly beautiful woman, five feet seven inches tall with long flowing blond hair, those big blue eyes, and a radiant smile. She was wearing blue jeans with strategically placed holes, a pink shirt with a long-sleeve button-down, worn unbuttoned and untucked over it. Way too pretty for a six-foot-four-inch 250-pound, old redneck like me.

We sat in a booth, ordered, and talked about everything you're not supposed to on a first date, politics, religion, and our ex's. We also talked about our kids. I was a single dad of two boys, and she was a single mom. She told me about her son and how she had also raised three of her sister's kids. I was impressed. Then she said the nine words that would forever change my life.

"Wow," she said. "You surprised me."

"Yeah, why?"

"Because you have a brain."

On October 19th, 2015, I fell in love.

Life goes on and between me working fifty-plus hours a week, killing home invaders with six legs or more, and Jennifer working almost eighty hours a week at night in the home healthcare and hospice field, we saw each other as much as we could. It had been almost thirty days since that fateful night. The woman I had zero expectations for was so much more than someone *I could date for a while,* as I first thought. I knew this was the woman God had made for me, but what could I do? I've been single for so long. A guy like me just doesn't fall in love overnight, does he? What would my boys say? How would the dogs react? Is this truly love? My heart says yes, but my head says be careful. The last time I listened to my head, it ended up costing me not only money but my self-respect. *Okay heart, you win.*

Jennifer came over before she went to work one night and told me was going up to South Carolina for Thanksgiving. My heart sank, and I didn't understand it. After all, I was a self-sufficient American male. But I couldn't stand the thought of her leaving me even for a week.

Jennifer's evil plan was in full swing, after all, she did tell me on our first date that "I needed a wife." The only problem was that she wasn't totally in control of her plan. She didn't expect me to jump into her snare with both feet, but I gladly let myself get caught.

Kissing her goodbye, surrounded by my "dead things," guns and arrows on my living room wall, I did the only thing I could, to ease my heart and mind, I blurted out, "So let's go look at rings on Saturday."

With a look that I would soon recognize, smiling and rolling her blue eyes. She said, "What? Daniel, are you crazy?"

With the roll of her eyes and the tone of her voice, I realized I had in fact lassoed a tornado and I better hold on tight.

Oh man, did I blow it? Looking for the right words to say, my throat was dry, I started to speak as she picked up her purse, but the words wouldn't come out.

"Honey, I have to go to work. Let's talk about this when I get back from my sister's. Okay?"

"Yeah, okay." I sighed. "No. I mean we have time now."

"Daniel?" Her eyes pierced my soul. "Are you serious?"

"Yes." Taking her hands in mine. "Jennifer, look I know it's fast, but I am so in love with you. We are made for each other."

Jennifer thought about it and said, "Okay?" uncertain of her answer. "I really have to get to work." Kissing me, she said, "Saturday? This Saturday?"

"Yes. This Saturday."

She smiled, shook her head as she got into her SUV, and said, "Okay. I love you too." She sighed, smiled, and put her car in reverse. Shaking her head again, "Saturday?" and backed out of my driveway.

Little did I know, Jennifer was as excited as I was. Although the night we met my expectations were zero, I was tired of being alone. A year or so earlier, I started to pray for a spouse. I thought my prayers were in vain. I was trying to force a relationship to happen. Because of that, I made several mistakes when it came to dating.

Jennifer was also praying, and she knew that God was going to answer her prayers. She just didn't expect it to happen in thirty days. After all her plan wasn't supposed to go into effect until January, but God's time isn't ours.

Saturday afternoon arrives. We hadn't seen each other since Tuesday night. My heart is pounding, what should I wear? A nice shirt, or just a tee. Is my hair combed? I was steady as a rock the day that I declared we were going to look at rings, and now I'm a train wreck. *Get it together Dan. You have to be cool.* I take a deep breath and decide on a black tee featuring one of my favorite guitar players.

A car door closed. She's here. "Oh boy," I whisper to the dogs, as my heart returned to pounding in my chest. *Calm down, play it cool.*

"Hey, good looking." I said as I walked outside "I missed you."

"Hey, yourself." She said, walking towards me with a kiss.

Jennifer came in the house and the dogs all wagged around her looking for some love. "Scoot your boots girls. Go lay down." She said, Boo, Sully, and Mikey, just looked at her and kept looking for a pat on the head.

"Git," I said, and they went and laid down. "Honey, they have lived with a redneck since they were born," I said laughing.

She looked beautiful. Jeans, heels, a tee-shirt with the ever-present button-down. Her hair flowing past her shoulders and those eyes. *Thank you, Lord.* She catches my gaze.

Smiling she said, "What?"

Shaking my head, I replied. "Nothing, honey. Are you ready?"

The drive to the mall, with her hand in mine, was a tense one. The only thing breaking the silence was the sound of a Blackberry Smoke CD. We would shoot each other sly glances every few miles. Although my confidence was coming back, the more I looked at her the more this felt like a dream. *Is she really real?*

Jennifer tried not to show how nervous she truly was. We'd known each other less than thirty days. She had good reason to be nervous. We both did. When she told her sister we were looking at rings so soon, Julie asked her if she was going to run. Jennifer said, "No." She knew something special was going here.

Parking the car, we got out and I gave her a kiss. Hand in hand we walked towards the door. Jennifer stopped mid-step, turns, and said, "Daniel, what are we doing here?"

"Like I said sweetie, buying a ring."

With a half-smile on her face and her blue eyes showing her true state of mind, she looked down. I grabbed her by the hand and lead her to the door. With every step, I saw this confident country girl's face go from uncertainty to fear.

Jennifer had never been married and until recently, she thought all men were... let's just say jerks. But she always had a spark for "That Guy."

Englewood, Florida was a nice small two-lane town twenty-five years ago. There were three bars, a dozen churches, one Publix, and we all knew the local police officers by name. That's when Jennifer first noticed a big guy with long black hair and beard. She thought he looked like a wild man. She just might have been right.

Jennifer is eight years younger, and when she was a cashier and bagger at Publix, there was something she found intriguing about "That Guy." Her name for me. When she bagged my groceries, she would insist on walking me out to my truck. She was very inquisitive, asking me all kinds of things. Questions like my boy's names, and what I did for a living? She never asked my name, I was "That Guy."

On our first date, she remembered Danny at five, his round little red face, and one-year-old Baley sitting in the cart. She remembered their names, and how "attentive" I was to my boys. Jennifer went on to tell me she would see me over the years and think to herself, *There's That Guy, I wish I didn't hate men so much.* During our conversation, she became very bold and told me "You need a wife." (The trap slams shut.) Apparently, she was right, because twenty-five years after our first meeting, here she is with "That Guy" buying wedding rings.

Walking into Kay Jewelers, our hands parted, and the look on her face was one of hesitation. Her eyes were wide and her mouth straight. Her hands were shaking and so was her voice. I didn't know if she's going to cry, run, or both.

As for me, my confidence was back and I'm strutting around like a rooster because the most beautiful girl in the world is going to be my wife. I can't believe how God has blessed me.

The man behind the counter approached us. He is five foot ten inches tall, 225 pounds, with slicked-back hair and a Hollywood white smile. "Welcome to Kay's, my name is John. How may I help you today?"

Jennifer said, "Umm."

"We're here to look for rings," I said.

Smiling "Congratulations." John said. "We have some lovely wedding sets right over here." Pointing to a long case that sparkles with diamonds and gold, "These start at five-thousand dollars."

I swallowed hard.

"No. I want something simple, but nice."

That's my girl. I thought.

"Oh okay," John said. Walking down the case. He stopped and said, "These start at one thousand dollars."

That's more budget-friendly.

Jennifer and I were pretty much in the same place financially. As a rule, single parents do not have a lot of disposable income. While raising kids, the money of a single parent goes to pay the bills and put food on the table. If you have a better than average job, then your children can have extras, like sports, new bikes, and some things that people take for granted. We were both lucky enough to have good jobs and our kids lacked for little. That doesn't mean we had a lot in the bank.

We are both very frugal, and Jennifer walked a little further down the case. She asked to see a few different sets of rings, but when she put on a white gold engagement ring and wedding band, her eyes sparkled, and a smile returned to her face.

"This is a beautiful set," John said.

"It is. What do you think, sweetheart?" I asked.

"It is beautiful," She said, "but I think we need to look at the other stores in the mall."

"Okay," I said. "John, can you hold these for us?"

Smiling that Hollywood smile he said, "Of course. But only until close of business today."

Looking at me, Jennifer said, "Thank you, very much, John."

"We will be back," I said as he handed me his business card.

We headed out into the mall hand in hand. Jennifer's face was less contorted with fear, but she was still trembling a little, she realized that her plan was working. With hundreds of people around us, kids laughing and running around, and the annoying kiosks barkers, we didn't hear a thing. As far as we were concerned the mall was empty. We were in a world of our own.

Strolling from store to store, my mind wandered. This is happening. What am I doing? What is she doing? We've only known each other for thirty days.

I remembered how twenty-seven days ago, I walked into that very Kay Jewelers. Not knowing why just knowing that I needed to show her how I felt. Jennifer has never taken off the cross and chain necklace I gave her. I knew right away that she was the girl for me, so why am I worried?

I caught her looking at me and smiling. *Stop over-thinking. Listen to your heart, not your brain. Shut up brain.* I squeeze Jennifer's hand as we walked into another jewelry store, but nothing caught her eye. Moving on, she finally found another ring she liked. Trying it on, she said, "What do you think?"

"It's nice honey, but you're the one wearing it."

Her eyes didn't sparkle as they did before. Sighing she said, "You're right."

It's decision time.

"Honey, why don't we get something to eat and talk a bit?"

"That sounds good." She said, "I would love a hot pretzel."

After getting our drinks and pretzel, we found a table and sat down. I looked into Jennifer's eyes and said, "Which ring do you like?"

Breaking eye contact, "I guess the one over there." Pointing to one of the jewelry stores in the mall.

"Really?" I said, "How come?"

"Well, it's pretty."

"Yeah, but your eyes didn't light up when you put it on."

Looking and smiling at me, "But I like it."

"Honey, do you like it because it's less expensive?"

"Yeah. I guess so."

Taking her hand in mine and coaxing her to meet my stare, "I told you money doesn't matter. I want you to have the one you want."

"I know," she said, "but..."

"No. There are no buts about it." Remaining silent, but looking at me, I continued, "Now which ring do you really want?"

"I really like the one in Kay's."

Taking the last sip of my drink, and gathering up our trash, we both stood and strolled into Kay's. Jennifer's face was as beautiful and confident as the night we met some thirty days ago. She had that certain saunter, the way her arms swung, her shoulders back, head held high, and that sparkle in her eye. She's back.

"Welcome back," John said.

Jennifer said with a smile. "Can I please see those rings again?"

"Of course, you can." John walks over to the counter and pulls out the set we were looking at. "Here you go."

Handing the rings to Jennifer, John gives me a wink, I smile back, he knows I hit the jackpot.

"What do you think Daniel?"

"I think that they are almost as beautiful as you."

"Oh, you just hush." She said with a bright smile.

"What matters is what do you think? Remember this is gonna last a long time."

"I love them." She said, "now let's look for your ring."

John breaks in and says, "You're also getting a ring?"

"Yes, I am. You can see how much jewelry I wear." Showing him my hands without as much as a hint of gold or silver on them.

"Well," He said, "I'm sure you will wear this for a long time. Follow me." He headed down to a smaller case, that still sparkled under the lights. Turning to Jennifer, "What are you looking for in a band for Dan?"

"He's a big guy, he needs a big band," Jennifer said. "I want to make sure everyone can see that he is taken."

"Okay then, a wide band," John said. Sizing me up he takes out a small keychain of rings. "Let's see what size you are." Taking a size ten out of the ring sizer, that didn't even go over my knuckle. "You do have some big hands, my man," John said. "Let's try this one." Size twelve. It went on but was tight. "Okay, this has got to be your size and put on a thirteen. "A perfect fit. Now, what are you looking for in a ring?"

Being raised in the outdoors, I have an affinity for everything camouflage. "I don't know, do you have a camo wedding band?" I said laughing.

John walked down the case and pulled out a camouflage wedding band. "This is a good seller with men." While he handed it to me.

My mouth was agape I was more than a little surprised. "I was only half kidding," I said.

"Do you like it?" Jennifer asked.

"Yeah, I do, but it's not what I want to wear as your husband," I said. "I want something as special as you."

We looked through all the rings, besides the camouflaged one, there were fancy engraved rings, rings with diamonds, and even a wedding band that matched my tattoo with skulls. I chose a simple white gold band that closely matched Jennifer's rings.

"Are you sure you don't want the camouflaged one? Jennifer asked.

I looked at her, and said, "Yes, honey, I'm sure."

"Alright, but why? You have everything in camo."

Thinking for the right words to explain why I didn't want a camouflage ring, I said, "Jennifer, this isn't a new hat, shirt, or even a new shotgun. This is my wedding ring. This ring is a sign of our love for each other, and I don't want to hide that."

Jennifer gave me that look again and hugged me tight.

"Then this is the ring?" John asked.

"That's the one," I said.

"Good choice," John said, "today we are running a sale on all of our wedding rings."

"Really?" Jennifer asked.

"Yes," John said. "So, this is what we're going to do, Dan, you are going to buy two of your rings..."

"But I don't need two rings."

"Dan," he said. "Just listen,"

"Good luck with that," Jennifer said.

Smiling, John continued, "Like I was saying you buy two of your rings and the set for Jennifer. This way you have enough points to get Jennifer's rings for free."

Now I was a little shell shocked from the day, the reality of what we were doing finally set in and my self-assurance was once again fleeting. "Okay," I said. "Then what?"

"I'm glad you asked," John said. "When the rings come in, you keep one ring and I send the other one back and refund your money for one of your rings and Jennifer's set."

"Is that legal?"

"Of course, it is," John said. "Besides, you two are a cute couple, and I don't mind helping you out a little."

This just didn't make sense to me. "So, I pay for two of my rings, and Jennifer's rings, and then what?"

He explained how their reward points work. That we would get Jennifer's engagement ring and her wedding band and my ring, just for the price of my wedding ring.

John smiling his Hollywood smile, said, "Do you understand?"

"No."

"Thank you," Jennifer said. "How do we get something engraved in the ring?"

"We will take care of that after the rings get back from being sized. But what do you want it to say?"

"Easy," I said.

"Easy?" He asked.

"Yes," Jennifer said, "Because our love is easy."

Smiling, John said, "That's sweet."

"It's true," I said. "I've never experienced anything like a love that feels so right."

"That's because we both prayed for a spouse," Jennifer said. "We believe that God has truly brought us together."

Nodding my head, in agreement.

"Nice" John said. "Now, how would you like to pay for this today?"

Waking out of the mall, her hand in mine, Jennifer said, "I can't believe we did it."

"Why?" I asked.

"Because it's all like a dream," she said.

"Yeah, like a nightmare?" I asked.

"Daniel, sometimes, I just don't know about you," Jennifer said smiling.

I stopped in our tracks, pulled on her hand, and spun her back to me, pulled her into me looked into her captivating blue eyes kissed her, and said, "Jennifer, I love you like I love my dogs. No, even more. And that is saying something." I said smiling.

She smacks me in the arm and said, "I love you too. You weirdo."

On December 12, 2015, in my living room with the dogs watching and surrounded by my "dead things," guns and arrows on my wall, I asked Jennifer Joy Gibbons to be my wife. February 26, 2016, four months and seven days after that fateful night in October, we were married. Though we have had many challenges over the past six years, our love and marriage has always been easy. Like Jennifer says, "Life is hard, but marriage is easy."

Lost & Found

by M.R. Shorey

"So, what school did you go to last year?" I asked Ginny, who was sitting on the swing next to mine. We had each picked that spot because it was the best place to check out all the new boys as the buses brought them in from the outlying schools.

"Dizzy Six. You?"

"The old Charlottesville schoolhouse."

"Ew! Isn't that the one with the outhouses built inside right at the back of the classroom? Must have smelled like an outhouse."

"Well," I answered in defense of the one-room schoolhouse, "it wasn't all that bad—except for the coal-burning stove. It was huge—at least six feet high and I don't know how big around. Now, that smelled! If we got our coats wet in the snow, we had to wear them and stand right next to that big old stove until they were dry. The whole place smelled like wet wool. Worse yet was when Mrs. Benton started the coal fire first thing each morning. The whole room smelled like a rotten egg!"

Ginny burst out laughing. "You mean it smelled like farts! That's what you have to put up with when you go to a school with indoor outhouses."

I started to laugh, too. Couldn't help it. "We can't talk like baby sixth graders anymore. Sixth graders say farts. We say . . . um . . . uh . . . passes gas." In spite of the effort to appear more grown up, our laughter gave us away as first-day-in-The-Central-School kids. Last year's sixth graders. We had to remember what a big step we had just taken. We were now with the big kids—from the eighth graders to the seniors—all in one school. In our minds that truly made us grownups.

"Why would the school send us to its worst, oldest buildings?" asked Ginny. "And they're all so far away, we have to ride school buses to get to them. All those buses and bus drivers must cost enough to build a new school."

"My dad says it's because of the new atomic power labs. They need a lot of scientists. The scientists move here with their families, and their kids take up more seats than we have in the central school, so they use those old schools that have been just sitting around empty."

"'Besides,' Dad always adds, 'What's so bad about going to a school where you can pet and feed beautiful horses every recess?'"

Changing the subject, I asked Ginny, "How come you call the District Six school Dizzy Six? Doesn't sound much better than where I went."

"Just to make fun of it. Actually, it's not much better than Charlottesville. The plumbing is about the same. No, a little better. We can hand pump our own water right in the front yard. And, get this, we had horses near us, too. They waited for us to come and feed them. We gave them the fruit and vegetables from our lunches. They liked to eat them, we didn't, and our mothers thought we were eating everything they packed."

We both stopped chatting as the bus pulled in carrying this year's new students from near Scotia. We riveted our attention on the opening door to check them out—the boys, that is. One in particular caught my interest. Actually, it was his hair that caught my interest. It was curly—beautifully curly. Not fair! The guys get the curls, and the girls have to resort to bobby pins. As he descended the steps inside the bus, his hair looked sort of brown. But the minute he stepped into the sunlight; each perfect curl radiated the most golden, glowing blond color I had ever seen. Oh, my!

I hoped, hoped, hoped he would be assigned to the same homeroom. With sixty-odd seventh graders entering the central school, we would be split in two different groups.

My mind raced on through the maybe list. Maybe his last name fell alphabetically close to mine? Better chances of being seated next to him. Every Friday gym class was dancing class, partners randomly assigned. Maybe we would be partnered up. Electives. Do seventh graders take electives? Maybe I could find out which electives he chose, and take the same? Maybe.

The maybe list was interrupted by a glaring, logical question: What's the attraction? Hair? Only hair? Time to get real. Time to watch the rest of the people on the bus from near Scotia. Time to watch for the other buses. Time to become a seventh grader. Time to meet my homeroom teacher.

Our homerooms were both in the basement just off the cafeteria. We called them the dungeons. Not far from wrong. A smiling well-fed lady greeted us. "Good morning. Welcome to Central School. My name is Miss Horst. Please take your seats in alphabetical order. Those whose names begin with A start at the door, followed back in the same row with B names . . ." My seat was at the end of the next to last row, in the next to last seat. From there I could look out through one of the small ground-level windows and see part of a parking lot. What I could not see from there was the boy with curly brown hair that reflected the sun as golden blond.

Miss Horst walked each aisle, individually greeting every student and handing them their schedules. Once done, she instructed, "Those of you going to English class, please stand up." She gave directions and sent them on their way. I was in the third group to leave the room.

History was my first class. It was with Mr. Davis. He had a surly expression and curly hair—only his hair was gray and let a lot of sunshine reflect off his scalp. He was prepared with a list of our names and shouted us to our seats. "Miss Gail Agnew!" "Mr. Glenn Baker!" "Miss Eleanor Charles!" . . . and so on until everyone was seated.

Mr.? Miss? I know Central School was for the older students, but really—Mr. and Miss? The one with the curly hair was there and to my disappointment, learned his name was Rob Ferris. No, I wasn't disappointed his name was Ferris, but that it started with an F, a long way from the S of my last name.

The next class was Science with Mr. Bernard who told us to take any seat we wanted. "Just don't fill up the back row first."

I headed for some middle-of-the-room desk when I saw Rob Ferris walk in. He headed straight for the front of the room. It was then I noticed he was wearing glasses. Perhaps he sat up front to see the board better. I quickly changed direction from the middle to the front of the room and sat. Guess where? To Rob's immediate left. And for no reason other than beautiful hair.

I felt the beginnings of my very first crush.

I looked down at the printed class schedule and pretended to be studying it. I was actually studying the exact position of my head and eyelids and analyzing how they must look. I slowly turned my eyes toward Rob, being ever so careful to keep my eyelids in their studying-the-paper-on-the-desk shape and hold my head perfectly still. Over time I perfected the art. I came to recognize his handwriting. He had an odd way of forming his G's and an almost backward method of writing his O's. He always wrote with a lead pencil. The eraser didn't look used. Did he never make a mistake? He faithfully wrote down the homework that was assigned and came to class with it completed—neatly and correctly.

Through junior and senior high, being in the same classes and activities with Rob was pretty much the luck of the draw. Though we were both into track and probably the best on our teams, the girls' and boys' teams never practiced together or went to the same meets. No time together there. We both got into the Drama Club. He was usually the stage manager, and I was usually in the cast. Other than telling me to stop talking in the wings, we rarely spoke to each other. In the classes we both attended, we usually sat near each other. Or, more accurately, I made sure to get a seat near his.

Now, Latin I and Latin II were different, each from the other. Rob and I were in separate Latin I classes, and the year went quickly for me. Miss Romano took us patiently through conjugations, and declensions and a fairly simple vocabulary. I still remember "Veni, vidi, vici."

But Latin II was different in every way. First, Rob was in the same class. Second, from day one and our teacher's assignment to translate: "All Gaul is divided into three parts," I knew I was in over my head. That turned out to be a blessing in disguise, though. Through the whole year of troublesome translations, I regularly asked Rob for help. And he gave it. He was a pretty darned good teacher. He knew his Latin—every word we were ever taught. Oh, it's heaven to be in over your head.

My very first crush, the crush on Rob Ferris, began that first day of seventh grade as he got off the bus. It grew with each passing year. Sometimes I believed—hoped—it went both ways. Other times I thought it was all in my head, and I never crossed his thoughts. I wish I could count on the daisies to know for sure. He loves me? He loves me not?

The closest thing we had to a date all started with a bit of lunch time conversation and a taunt. Rob was overheard talking about the bobsled he was making out of skis and ropes or whatever.

"It'll never work," taunted Mike.

"Wanna bet?"

"Yeah."

Rob ended it with great confidence "Bet's on, and you'll be on the first run if you're brave enough to ride a bobsled that'll 'never work.'"

"We'll see. Let me know when you're done," said Mike as he threw his empty lunch bag in the trash.

Shortly after the first good snowstorm, Rob announced the bobsled's initiation. "Meet me near the big hill behind the Mayflower Plaza this Saturday." Besides Mike, he invited me and another girl, Rhonda, to make a team of four.

On the day of the ride, it was windy and bitterly cold. We all helped haul the bobsled into place. Was it heavy! And it didn't look quite like any I had seen before. Rob had fastened two sets of skis (one sawed off set for the front with the tips still on and one set for the back, sawed off at both ends).

"Makes it easier to steer," Rob explained as he sat down at the very front.

"How fast does this thing go?" asked Mike.

"Not sure. It's the first time. Depends on our weight, how slippery the slope is, and a couple of other things."

By now, the bobsled was starting to slide, and we were piling on behind Rob.

"Where are the brakes?" Mike shouted.

All we heard of the answer was, "Brakes?" The rest was lost in the wind. The sled was already flying down the hill.

Faster and faster it flew. Rhonda and I started to scream—partly for fun and partly from fear. What else had Rob said about the brakes?

Mike joined the yelling. But his voice held only fear. We were headed straight for a barbed wire fence.

On top of the yelling and screaming, we heard Rob's voice: "DUCK!"

We did, and just in time. Miraculously, we weren't decapitated.

The bobsled eventually stopped.

"What was that you said about the brakes?" asked Mike suspiciously.

"I said," answered Rob, "'the brakes work when you start going up a slight rise.'"

"This hill doesn't have a slight rise in the direction we were going," observed Mike.

We lugged his bobsled back up the hill. It was heavier than before, and the hill was longer going up than it was going down. By the time we reached the top, we were too exhausted and too wise to go down again.

I came home with a smile on my face and frostbite on my thighs. Our first date?

It was not unusual to attend the same parties, play the same party games, sometimes with Rob, but nothing ever matched flying down the hill on the bobsled.

Then came June of 1956—graduation. Rob won the Latin Medal, among many others, and a four-year scholarship to Johns Hopkins. I received a couple of minor honors, though I don't even recall what they were for. Then, with the switch of the tassels from right to left, it all came to an end, and we each went our separate ways: he went to Baltimore to become a physicist; I went to Buffalo to become a teacher.

As the years passed, my crush on Rob was no more than a few memories without the emotions they once held. Our paths never crossed. He didn't get to any class reunions, though news of him did. He married and started a family. I married and started a family. I got a divorce.

More years passed. I remarried and along came the computer. With it eventually came e-mail. Every once in a while, I heard from Rob. He and his wife had visited the Rhododendron Gardens. They got a new golden retriever. They moved.

One year, I decided to pay off the mortgage before I reached 100. Then before 90. Then before 80. Then (ta da!) as soon as possible, and I went on an austerity budget. It was a contest of wills between me and the world. Every expense was cut to the bone. What was the cheapest nutritional breakfast? Where were the nearest thrift stores? How long could I make the tires last? How late in the year could I turn on the furnace? Nothing was sacred except for coffee. That was my one and only extravagance—Skinny Guy's freshly roasted and ground special coffee. Twelve dollars a pound and worth every penny of it. Right after I got into the new budget, my computer crashed, so I did without one for a couple of years. Mortgage first.

More years passed. Paid off the mortgage, bought another computer, Skinny Guy closed. I was unprepared for the let-down of paying off the house. It was almost like grief. I had also lost contact with Rob. I did get an e-mail supposedly from him, but knew it was a fake. It was full of misspelled words and bad punctuation. Rob was a class brain, and class brains don't make mistakes like the sender did. Sigh! My very first crush was now lost forever. Oh, well.

The end of the century came and went. Then came 2019 and the start of COVID-19. Life as we knew it was yanked out from under us. Face masks, social distancing, empty spaces on the grocery shelves, no restaurants open, Zoom was the new face-to-face, no hugs. I actually saw only three people, and that was outside on either their patios or mine sitting waaaaay far apart. We brought our own drinks, not sharing them with others. Strangest year, strangest life. Then on the Fourth of July of the strangest year, I received an e-mail from Rob. In part it read, "I am now living in Seattle, Washington with my daughter. I am fairly mobile."

Fairly mobile? That's a rather small thing, but a good thing. Fairly mobile translates to not very mobile. I've lost my sense of balance and walk like a bent over drunk. So, my not-very-mobile won't look so bad next to his not-very-mobile. Living with his daughter? Now, that's a big thing and revs up my curiosity. What about his wife? Passed away? In a nursing home? Suffering from COVID-19? Though it was my most burning question, I answered his e-mail without asking the question. A couple of short lines of chit chat was all I sent back. Three or four days later, he answered. Just generalities.

Soon, an e-mail was going back or forth each day. Though I now wanted to keep in touch with him as a friend, I still figured we were so far apart, we would stick to e-mails instead of getting together. We both hated flying, and the distance was too long for people our age to drive. Neither of us had friends or family in each other's home states. And that was just the beginning of the list. Though the idea of a visit appealed to me, I realized it was not a reality.

Our e-mails were more frequent now. One from him each day, and one back the same day. We covered everything from old memories to making sourdough bread to bucket lists. He wanted to find a log cabin in the woods near a stream and started sending me pictures of cabins and other homes in his area from Zillow. I wanted to finish a book I had been working on for four years and sent him some of the finished chapters. He was such pleasant "company" during these unending days of solitude.

One day the topic of family came up, and it turned out there were two generations of his family living less than a half hour's drive from my door. He began talking about a visit here if he could figure a safe way to do so during COVID-19 times—to see family, of course. I hoped with family so close, he would include a visit to me.

"Just in case, I'd better start cleaning house. I've got to get rid of stuff." I told my neighbor, Dana. "There's so much junk to get rid of. What do you think of a yard sale?"

"Great idea! I can bring plenty of stuff if you don't have enough."

Don't have enough? That's a laugh, I thought.

"We can do it together. It would be fun!" I got caught up in her enthusiasm and set the dates.

COVID-19 made yard sale safety a challenge. We spent the rest of the time figuring everything we could possibly do. Ask for exact change. Saturate money with alcohol. Give only sanitized money for change. Every sign should have these three words: "SALE" and "MUST MASK." We thought of everything. We even decided on putting a full-size skeleton out front holding a sign: "Please mask. I didn't."

I gathered bags and boxes of former treasures. Rob had just bought a new car and set a date for driving it here. Oh dear. My yard sale was going to be right in the middle of his local visit, and the house was far into the looking-worse phase and nowhere near the looking-better part. Oh help!

The getting ready time was shrinking, and my stress was growing. It was Tuesday. Only three days to get ready for the sale and four until Rob's arrival. An early deep freeze was predicted, and I had to rescue the vegetables.

It was the day Rob started his drive here. I was in the beauty parlor about to have my hair cut. "Let me go sanitize your chair. I'll be back in one minute," said the beautician as my phone rang. It was Rob.

"I'm afraid I can't make it. Forest fires surround miles of the road down from Seattle, and the traffic is crazy. I'm going to have to turn around."

The beautician was waiting to take me to the chair. "Rob, I'm sorry to interrupt, but I'm headed for a haircut this very minute. Can I call you tonight?"

"Sure. Talk to you later," he answered, and we both hung up.

Haircut done, I went home, brought in the vegetables, and fixed dinner. Totally drained, I glanced outside as I sat down with my son Dan, and saw a night filled with snow. Beautiful! It obscured the roof of my neighbors' house. At the same time, a car pulled into the drive. Lost in the snow? "Dan, is that anybody you know?"

"Nope. I thought it was one of your friends."

We continued to watch as a scraggly-haired, unkempt man got out and reached into the car to get something from the back seat.

"I'll take care of it," Dan offered as he threw on a jacket and went out to defend the homestead.

Minutes later, a snow-covered Dan came back in with a bouquet, a plastic bag containing a small box, and a wide smile.

"If this is from the person I suspect it's from, Rob must think you are really mad at him."

I laughed at the idea, put the bouquet in the living room and took the box from the plastic bag. It was candy—chocolate truffles.

"Dessert," Dan and I said at the same time.

We finished dinner including a couple of truffles as the snow piled up. And it was only mid-September.

I called Rob and thanked him for the flowers and the candy. Suspecting Dan's remark had merit, especially after I practically hung up on Rob, I assured him I wasn't upset. "Rob, things happen. There'll be safer times for traveling. I don't want you even wondering if I'm upset. Sure, I'm disappointed. I had been looking forward to seeing you." I'm not sure he believed me. We talked a bit longer and said good night.

I turned the patio lights on and sat on the couch where I could watch the snow fall. Though I love the snow—even shoveling it—it was making my yard sale impossible.

Impossible? Yes, that's exactly the right word! Having the yard sale this week is impossible. Go along with it, girl!

Suddenly everything I had fretted over fell like dominoes. I got the haircut. I saved the vegetables. I had another week to get ready for the sale. I didn't have to spiff up the house yet for Rob and whichever family member brought him here. With each domino that fell, I felt relief. The weight of the world was lifted from my shoulders. What a peaceful ending to such a hectic, stressful day. Thank you, snow.

The next morning, I e-mailed Rob and complimented him on the wisdom of his turning back and avoiding the foot-plus deep snow left by the storm. I knew he believed me this time.

After our earliest recorded snowstorm, it went back to being fall. Fall turned into winter. After all this time, I still didn't have a clue about Rob's feelings for me. By the end of December, I decided that if nothing changed by the new year, it would be time to slowly back away from the constantly alternating signals.

The latest phone call from Rob was a typical "confuser" and brought reruns of school days. Back to the old "He loves me. He loves me not." If only I had an accurate daisy to pluck—then or now.

"I forwarded info on another Zillow house for sale," he began, "would you take a look at it for me? You'll like it—especially the whole wall of bookshelves with a rolling library ladder. If you want, I'll buy it." He paused, then chuckled and added, "You furnish it, though."

He'll buy it and I'll furnish it? I'll like the wall of book-shelves? As a whole, it sounded like he was planning a life together, but nowhere was one single romantic word. He loves me. He loves me not. Here we go again!

"I don't feel comfortable being the one to decide. How about this? I like it, you fly down and look it over before you commit to it?"

"Sounds sensible. Would you feel better if you got another opinion first?"

"Absolutely!"

"All right. I'll call my son Lloyd to do the walk-through with you. He'll be as critical as I would be since he's getting the house when I'm gone. If he thinks I should buy it, I'll fly down."

Lloyd and I met for the first time in front of the property. I had taken a wrong turn and arrived late. That must have made a great first impression, an airhead who can't get anywhere on time. Late—late is rude. A rude airhead.

What if Lloyd thought Rob should buy the place? And Rob flew in with COVID-19 so rampant? Overcrowded hospitals, equipment shortages, front liners' physical and emotional stamina running close to empty. That alone made Rob's traveling doubly questionable. Traveling was a bad option—especially by air. I hope Lloyd doesn't like the place.

He didn't. Whew!

The relief was only temporary. In less than twenty-four hours Rob sent more possible places to look at. It was getting easier to veto them as we shortened the list of must haves and expanded the list of don't wants.

The housing market was crazy with bidding wars waging, houses bought sight unseen, properties sold the day they went on the market, some within hours. Prices were skyrocketing—up twenty percent.

Because of all that, and despite COVID-19, Rob decided to fly down right away—in just five days. And the old question reared its ugly head: What if we don't like each other? What will I see? What if I don't like his manners? His jokes? His gray hair? What if?

December 31, 2020, 12:00 noon. Rob called and in less than a minute, my life turned on a dime.

"I just looked at a house on Zillow and sent it on to you. I really like it. I'll buy it if you like it, but only if you live there with me. And I'm going to ask you to marry me."

My answer was a loooong silence. It's impossible to talk with your mouth hanging open.

Finally, "What . . . What if . . . What if we don't like each other? We haven't seen each other in sixty-five years."

"Then we both back out. No hard feelings. We'll still be friends."

An hour later, I sat staring into space, trying to find just one coherent thought in all the cacophony. Along with the what-if-he-doesn't-like-me question, ran the music in my head from The Man of La Mancha. What if Rob, now my man of La Mancha, believed he was about to see Dulcinea for the first time (in sixty-five years), and when he got close up, he saw Aldonza?

Till today, he occasionally said something flirtatious or used some term of endearment. Once, I responded in kind. Big mistake. He never made any reference to his words or my response. It was as if they had never existed. Embarrassed, I reined in my growing feelings and reminded myself, He's just a friend. But today that changed so quickly I was still dizzy from my turn on that tiny dime.

He immediately made plans to fly here and find "our" house—if we liked each other. Time would tell. As I went to greet him, I wondered: Dulcinea or Aldonza? He apparently didn't see either one. He saw an 82-year-old lady with well-earned wrinkles, a slight stagger, and a huge smile. I saw a man my age, wrinkled, a bit of a limp, and a huge smile.

But he must have also seen what I saw—an evasive, shadowy image of a once youthful schoolmate with the same twinkle of the eye.

The realtor we were working with found Rob a nearby B&B—two bedrooms, two baths, living and dining rooms, kitchen and over a thousand wonderful books.

He came over for breakfast at 9:00 sharp each morning with his laptop for us to pour over the houses on the market and pick the possibles. We spent the rest of the day doing walk-throughs or driving around checking different areas. In the car we shared old times and old memories. It's funny how two people can have such clear but differing memories of the same event. He remembered my taunting him about his bobsled. I remember Mike being the culprit. He says I was. He claims I fed him pablum at a party. News to me.

Interestingly, during the intervening years, we had often lived relatively close to each other, had gone to the same restaurants, museums, parks, and churches, yet never crossed paths. I learned that he had been keeping track of my whereabouts from time to time. Circumstances were okay for Christmas cards and occasional e-mails.

We saw so many houses, they began to blur, and we thought "our" house didn't exist. Then suddenly things fell into place. Between 8:30 and 11:00 on a Sunday morning, we heard about, saw, liked, and made an offer on a house. Even with a small glitch, our offer was accepted before lunch.

Then the real work began. In early March, we began the process of fitting two households into one house. In April, we wondered if it were possible. In May, we arranged to have an addition built. In June, the footings were poured. The house is filled with unpacked boxes, and we're having our first out-of-town visitor in just five days.

From March to today, our lives have gone from hectic to more hectic.

We keep asking each other, "Is this retirement?"

"Is this what 83-year-olds are supposed to be doing?"

HOW I MET MY OTHER

We hold hands to help each other as we limp and totter up inclines and stairs. We constantly ask each other, "Why are we moving big rocks to landscape the yard and climbing ladders to paint ten-foot-high rooms? Why?"

"Because we have 166 years of experience." says he.

"Because we want to," says I.

"Because we waited so long," we both say as we hold hands a bit more tightly and climb one more step.

Smitten

by Mona Posinoff

I wasn't looking for a relationship. I had finally become comfortable and even happy being single after an emotional and tumultuous break up with a long-time partner. Several years had passed. I dated a bit and reconciled myself to not having a special someone in my life, and that was okay. I lived in my own house in a small town in Massachusetts. I had my work, my community, hobbies, and best of all, my bicycling buddies.

Joining BLAB, Bicycling Lesbians Around Boston, was one of the best decisions I made after the breakup. The group formed a few years before I came to it. Some of the original members were still involved, while each spring brought newcomers. There were a range of ages and abilities, long and short rides, from spring through fall. Once colder bone chilling temperatures arrived, bikes were put away for the season.

Tuesday nights were shorter two-hour rides close to the immediate Boston city limits. Those rides averaged ten-fifteen miles, giving us lots of time to talk as we ped-dled at a slower speed through the traffic and lights of the surrounding communities. Each time we went out we usu-ally paired up with someone who rode at our pace so that we could talk as we peddled.

Saturdays were a longer ride, usually all day, meeting early in the morning west of the downtown city area in more country and farmland settings. These rides were scheduled by a 'lead' person who charted out the course and planned for lunch and snack breaks.

By my third year of riding with the Blabbers, I was a sea-soned leader. I lived the farthest west of the city folk, close to apple and pear orchards snuggled in among the hilly farm-land framed by quiet tree-laden back country roads. We all had our favorite routes and looked forward to new areas to explore. I was excited on this particular April Saturday morning to be riding with many of the core members who were my friends, as well as with one or two new attendees.

Standing in the MetroWest train parking lot, bicycles removed from the back or tops of vehicle racks, we made small talk waiting for all the riders to assemble.

"Do you know someone named Harley?" I asked. "She emailed that she had just joined and Katie referred her to me as the contact for this ride."

Lauren retorted, "I hope she knows it is bicycling and not motorcycling with a name like Harley."

We all laughed and watched as another car pulled into the small lot with a blonde woman at the wheel. We could see the tell-tale familiar style bike jersey showing on her shoulders.

Lauren whispered, "Do you think that's her? She doesn't look like a Harley." No, I thought, she doesn't look like a motorcycle mama.

I waited until the driver killed her ignition, and then approached the vehicle as the woman emerged, in full bike shirt, padded bike shorts and ankle socks—traditional bike uniform. Her chin length blonde hair highlighted her brown eyes and bright smile. Tight spandex bicycle shorts can make one look fat. This wasn't true for her. She looked every bit the fit athlete.

"Are you Harley?" *She's too attractive to be a 'Harley' but you never know*, I thought to myself. *Don't judge a book by its cover.* "Are you here for the BLAB ride?"

"Harley? No. My name is Ellie. I emailed someone last night about today's ride, and they told me to meet the group here. Am I in the right place?"

"Yes, this is where we're starting this morning," I replied. "Welcome. My name is Mona, and I'm leading today's ride. Glad you could make it. We'll get started in a few minutes if you want to get your bike ready," I told her. "We'll meet over there." I gestured to the area most of the others were standing with their bikes.

"Sounds good," she said. I turned around to return to the group.

"Is that Harley?" Lauren asked.

Ellie walked up to the group with her sleek thin-tired racing bicycle. Smiling, she introduced herself. "Hi, I'm Ellie." No shyness about this woman. She would fit right in. Everyone welcomed her and told her their names.

"There will be a test to see how many names you can remember," Lauren teased her. There were seven other core riders assembled today.

"We're going to be riding out towards Sudbury and Concord, with a lunch stop at Verrill farm stand in Concord. Let's have fun!"

Helmets and gloves on, we mounted our bicycles and started peddling single file until we got on one of the closer country roads where we could spread out. I always relished the first minutes of starting out on a bike ride. The feel of the seat beneath me, hands gripping the handlebars, legs beginning to pump, feet pushing and pulling the peddles. I was one of the few who still used regular bike peddles with cages, unlike the fancier bikes with clip-on shoes and peddles. I rode a hybrid bicycle—heavier tires than the racing bikes of my cohorts, heavier framed too. I definitely wasn't the fastest rider, but I could keep up at a steady pace.

Soon we were on the smooth back roads canopied by huge oaks and maples that lined the streets. I loved these Saturday morning rides and for some reason, today felt extra special. I couldn't have explained it at the time, but in retrospect I know why.

Ellie was a strong rider and soon was up front riding faster and at the head of our group. *She may be new to our group but she is a solid rider.* I willed my legs to go faster to catch up with her. I felt compelled to try to talk to her. After all, this was a BLAB ride.

"You're a fast rider," I said to her, almost out of breath. "You must ride a lot," I said.

"I used to when I lived in Texas. I just moved to Massachusetts a few months ago."

"What brought you here?" I asked

"My job. I was relocated even though I told them I really didn't want to live somewhere cold." She laughed. "They promised me they would move me to a warmer climate as soon as something opens up."

"What do you do?"

She proceeded to tell me about her work while we rode in tandem. She had slowed her peddling as we continued to converse. She said she hadn't met many people to do things with during the winter, but now that spring was here, she hoped to get out more. Listening to her talk I was conscious of the birds chirping in the trees we passed. The green manicured lawns with newly blooming perennials were a beautiful backdrop for this conversation. I inhaled deeply. Yes, this was a good day.

"What else do you like to do besides bike?" I asked her.

"Hike, run, visit new places. I'm hoping to meet more folks to be active with."

Since she was new to the state and area, I told her about a music house party I was going to that night, thinking she may be interested. "There'll be lots of women there, if you would like to attend. It's only $10.00 and should be fun. I can call and see if there's still space."

I really had no ulterior motive. I believed I was inviting her because she was new and it would be a good way to meet more people. "I can get your phone number when we get back to our cars," I told her.

"Sounds good," she said, and then peddled faster so she was off on her own. I rode with a few of the other cyclists, and soon we reached our halfway point and stopped at the local farm stand for our lunch break.

Standing around eating and snacking always leant itself to conversation. Recently I had been with a different group of friends where someone had a joint that we passed around. It had been a long time since I had gotten high. For some reason I decided to ask the group a question.

"Did you ever get high or do drugs?"

Some said yes, a few noes, and Ellie said never, plus she worked for a pharmaceutical company with mandatory drug testing. *Open mouth and insert foot.* Having been a child of the 60's and 70's and coming from Queens, New York, it was an innocent enough question. Maybe not.

Arriving back at the starting parking lot, we said our goodbyes. I reminded Ellie about this evening. "I'll get you one of my cards," she said. I walked my bike over to her car and waited while she dug around looking for her wallet. She removed a business card and wrote her home phone number on the back. Handing me the card, she said "This was a great ride. I'll look forward to tonight." Oh my! Was it a date? Was she saying she liked me? I didn't know what to think, but my stomach felt the butterflies flitting about.

Driving home, I reviewed our conversation. I liked her voice and found her attractive. I haven't felt this way in a long time. "Don't jump ahead of yourself," my inner voice of caution warned. "But, maybe it's time to allow a new person in," my support voice pushed back. I decided to listen to the positive and smiled inwardly at the possibility of this evening's meeting.

When I called Ellie's number, it went to voicemail. I was a little disappointed to not speak to her directly. Yes, my infatuation was growing. I left the message to call me for the address and directions. I proceeded to walk my dog, shower, eat, and wait on her call.

When she called, I was ecstatic but didn't let on. We agreed to meet at the house party.

Upon arrival, I asked my friend Inna if an attractive blonde woman had appeared yet.

"I don't think so, but I can't wait to meet this person who seems to have you smitten," she laughed and winked.

I found a seat on the sofa next to a couple I knew. We made small talk while I watched the doorway for Ellie. When she entered the living room, she immediately came over and sat on the other side of me. She had a great smile, bright white teeth, kind and laughing eyes. She was wearing blue jeans with a tailored shirt, and I was liking what I saw.

We made small talk. Did she have trouble finding it, etc. Then the musicians were introduced and began to play acoustic guitar and sing. We sat and listened. I was extremely aware of the closeness of our bodies and kept inching away and towards the other couple sharing the sofa. I had been badly burnt with my last ten-year relationship. Even though it had ended four years prior, the scars ran long and deep. That relationship had started as a one-night stand that turned into what I thought was finding my soulmate and living happily ever after. Until she left me for a much younger woman and that story book ending was not to be. I had dated a few women since, but none that felt like this.

Oh dear, I thought. *I think I like her.*

The music stopped. "We'll take a fifteen-minute break. There's soft drinks and snacks in the kitchen."

"Would you like something to drink?" I asked Ellie.

"Water would be great," she replied. "I need to stretch my legs. I'll go with you."

We both walked into the small but clean and organized kitchen.

Holding our cups of water, we stood opposite each other at the kitchen island and agreed we liked the songs even though we never heard these singers before. Ellie was well spoken, had a quick laugh, and yes, to use Inna's term, I was *smitten*.

"A few of us are going out dancing at the women's bar tonight. Would you like to join us?" I asked.

"Sounds like fun. I haven't been out dancing in a long time," she responded.

We returned to our seats, and I moved even closer to the friend on the other side of me to keep my distance from Ellie. *I think I like her and it scares me*. It had been a long time since I was attracted to someone who I thought I might want to date.

A few more songs, concert over, signed CDs purchased, then time for the women's bar and dancing.

"How 'bout I follow you? I still don't know my way around the city."

"Sounds good to me." I replied. The butterflies had returned. I was smiling, excited and nervous at the same time. As much as I wanted there to be 'something' between us, it scared me a little. I could feel the protective side of my heart trying to push through. I ignored it and made a conscious decision to stay with the warm feeling I had.

Parking in the underground garage, we took the elevator up to the top floor to the dance bar. Exiting the elevator, I asked her what she would like to drink.

"Jack Daniels and water."

"Okay, I'll get our drinks. You wait here."

I gave the bartender the order and thought, *She must be an alcoholic drinking something so strong. I guess we won't be dating.* I had my standards and one was no alcoholics or drug addicts. I was a social drinker only.

Walking back with a bottled beer for me and her tumbler of Jack in my other hand, we tipped our glass/bottleneck together and said: "To new friendship."

She sipped and didn't chug the drink, which I took as a good sign. Maybe there was hope after all.

The friends I was supposed to be meeting up with appeared and introductions were made. I asked Ellie to dance. Her body moved and swayed with the beat. I liked watching her. We continued to dance and I continued to be attracted to her. The loud music made it hard to talk, but each time she leaned in to me to say something, I could smell her perfume. It was rousing. The butterflies had flown off to be replaced by a warm and wanting feeling. I felt myself letting go and enjoyed being in the moment. Leaving the dance floor, we stood talking with my friends. It was getting late.

"It's been a long day. I'm ready to head home."

"Me too," she said, then added, "I'll walk you to your car."

As we approached the elevator, she suddenly turned and kissed me. Happily surprised, I returned the kiss. A flash of trying not to sit close to her at the concert blurred into wanting to hold her tightly and not let go.

"Well, I didn't see that coming, but I liked it," I said.

Again, that brilliant smile upturned her lips and added crinkles around her eyes.

"Me too," she said as we entered the elevator and then said goodbye at my car.

"I'll talk to you soon. Drive safe." She waved as I pulled slowly out of the garage watching her in the rearview mirror.

I was heady with that feeling. You know the one. Sort of like when you were younger and had your first crush on someone and you found out they liked you back? I hadn't felt this excited with possibility in a long time. I couldn't wait for her to call me. But, what if she didn't? What if she kissed all the girls she went out with? What would it be like to see her on a bike ride again having left me hanging? *SHHHHH,* I told the naysayer voices in my head. *Don't go there. Stay with the elation and thrill of having met someone new who is smart, personable, easy on the eyes and, who knows what else?*

She called the next evening.

I tried to sound friendly yet casual. *Go slow, take your time, let her lead,* I told myself. We started with small talk, telling each other how we spent the day. She asked me my sign.

"Aries. My birthday is the sixteenth."

"Perfect timing," she said. "I'd like to take you out for dinner for your birthday next Saturday night, if you're free."

Oh, calm my fluttering heart. "Actually, I'm having an Ellen Party on Saturday night with the BLAB women. You're welcome to come if you'd like." Ellen DeGeneres had come

Smitten

out a few years earlier on television and not everyone had seen that episode of her show. I had it on a VCR tape.

I heard the hesitation in her voice. "Could we do dinner on Friday night instead? I'll take a raincheck for the party."

"Friday night would be great, but it has to be a regular dinner. You're not taking me out for my birthday. You hardly know me." Secretly, I loved the idea of having her want to be with just me first before the whole group.

"You choose the restaurant since I'm sure you know more places than I do," she said.

"I can do that," I replied. "Do you like Indian food? It is one of my favorites and I don't get to eat it as often as I would like." This could be a make-or-break question I thought.

"Love it!" she answered enthusiastically.

"I know just the place in Harvard Square." I gave her the name of the restaurant and we decided to meet there at seven. The conversation continued for a good while until we both agreed it was time to say goodnight.

My birthday was the following Sunday. I was leading another ride, this time in my direct area, meeting just a mile from my house at the local supermarket parking lot. Depending on how dinner went on Friday night, maybe she would ride again? Either way, I was looking forward to this coming week, my birthday week. I had plans with friends three out of the next seven days. They all paled in comparison to the excitement I felt knowing I would be meeting Ellie on Friday night and maybe some smooching would be included.

Ellie called me mid-week to confirm our plans. We talked well over two hours. Conversation flowed easily and I liked listening to her voice and word choices. She was well spoken,

143

had a great sense of humor, and I found myself smiling through the telephone. It felt good to listen and exchange thoughts together.

Friday after work, I got home, walked my Lab mix rescue dog, then showered and tried on numerous shirts before deciding on my favorite cobalt blue silk with black jeans. A pair of earrings, non-ostentatious necklace, and I was off to meet this new stranger who I was interested in getting to know better.

And get to know her I did. I had a long list of questions for Ellie. When we refer back to that first dinner, she tells people she felt like it was the inquisition.

Sitting at the white clothed table for two with our glasses of water and merlot, I wanted to know everything about her. Neither of us had looked at the menus when the turbaned waiter handed them to us. Each time he returned to ask if we were ready to order, we turned him away with a "Need a few more minutes."

Finally, I told him, "When we're ready, I'll put the menus together at the edge of the table," a cue I worked with during the many years I waited tables earlier in my life.

As my friend Inna had said the weekend before, I was smitten. Who was this woman that just appeared out of nowhere and entered my biking life? My questions snow-balled towards her and she answered pragmatically. She was confident but not egotistical. She shared herself openly and seemed unencumbered. Oh my, I was liking her more and more with every syllable she uttered.

I found out where she was raised, how many siblings, what her family life had been like, where she'd gone to college and what she studied. What she did for work, past relationships, her goals, other hobbies, pets, favorite color, you name it. She passed the litmus test with flying colors.

Two hours later, we finally appeased the waiter and ordered. Thankfully, the restaurant hadn't been super busy that night so he didn't push us. We ate our meal slowly, a bite or two and lots of conversation in between. We were the last to leave the restaurant. It felt like we were in a bubble that advertised the fact this was a first get-to-know-each-other date and it was going well.

We decided to walk along the nearby Charles River. The evening air was cool, but not chilly. It could've been ten degrees and I wouldn't have noticed. I was too smitten.

Yes, some more kissing occurred. Lesbians used to be renowned for meeting, having sex, and moving in together immediately. Straight or gay, those kinds of relationships rarely last.

Something about this bicycling lesbian told me she was different. I knew I wanted to take it slow. I had been single for a while. I still had my guard up and didn't want to make a mistake I would regret. I had learned a great deal as a result of my last long relationship. Sex did not equal love. If I was going to recouple with someone, I wanted to know them first. My heart and body had a strong protective veneer that I had learned to respect. Talking and getting to know each other was upmost on my list. Kissing too. Sex, not for awhile.

We said our good nights and Ellie said she'd see me Sunday on the bike ride. I left feeling a huge YES!!!

The Saturday night BLAB gathering was a success and everyone wanted to know how my date had gone. I relished in the details of what I liked about Ellie. Those not on the first ride wanted to meet her.

"Let's see how it goes before you have me married off," I said.

Patience for all was the next step.

Awakening the next morning on Sunday, my birthday, I was filled with anticipation for the day. I have always liked my birthday in the northeast spring. The bright yellow of daffodils and forsythia, pink and red tulips, lime green sprouts of grass, leaves budding out on the awakening maples and oaks with the promise of warmer days—today was sure to be a good one.

I arrived at the meeting parking lot early. I had purposely selected a meeting place close to my house in Maynard. No one was there yet. The first car to show up was Ellie's. I walked over to greet her. We waited a while, almost a half hour, and then figured it was just us. Hmm, I wondered. Did 'the girls' stay away to give me and Ellie time alone? Hmmm.

"Do you still want to ride?" I asked her.

"Yes, I was looking forward to it."

"Okay, ride we will."

Off we went through the small towns of Stow, Acton, and Littleton. I always enjoyed riding and sharing these areas with others. Traffic was almost nonexistent on the one lane each way country roads. These towns exemplified old New England, west of Boston, with horse pastures and large green rolling hills set amid the stone wall fences. Ellie rode with me, at my pace. It was a pretty ride, only about thirty miles.

We ended back at the parking lot.

"Want to get some lunch?" she asked.

I looked at her and laughed. "You saw where we just rode. I live sort of in the middle of nowhere. The only restaurants open on a Sunday around here are fast food, and they are at least a twenty-minute car drive. I have some quiche leftover from last night if you want to come to my house. It's basically just around the corner."

As soon as I stopped talking, I wished I could've taken the offer back. Did I really want to be alone with Ellie in my house? One thing could lead to another and I did NOT want that to happen. *Okay, Mona. You can do this. Self-control will prevail,* I told myself.

She followed me in her car to my house. She had brought street clothes to change out of her bicycling ones. I showed her the bathroom and went upstairs to change, too.

After warming the broccoli and cheese quiche and preparing a quick salad, we sat down at the small rectangular wood kitchen table and ate. Finishing, I took the plates to the sink to wash. Ellie said she had something in the car and would be right back.

Walking back into the kitchen, she stated she got me a little something for my birthday.

"You hardly know me," I said. She held a shiny silver and gold gift wrapped jewelry looking box with a neat ribbon tied around it. She went to hand it to me.

Keeping my hands by my side, I said "That box looks like a piece of jewelry could be in it. I cannot accept jewelry from you."

Standing in front of me she retorted, "I enjoyed the other night and wanted to get you something. It's not a big deal. Just open it."

Had I learned somewhere to not look a gift horse in the mouth? I offered my hand and she placed the box in it.

My emotions were a flutter. She liked me enough to buy me something nice. What if it's ugly and I don't like it? What if it's really expensive? How can I accept it? What does this mean? It's only been a week, one real date, many phone conversations, and two bike rides.

My hands shook as I undid the ribbon, tore gift wrap, and noticed a jeweler's name embossed in black on the white outer box. Removing the lid, there was a light grey velvet covered box inside.

I pulled the cover up. Instantly I was in love with it—a one of a kind, beautifully simple wound silver open cuff bracelet with two small gold x's on it. The ends were wound with gold and finished neatly.

"Oh wow! It's beautiful," I told Ellie. "But I cannot accept it. It's too expensive a gift to give to someone you hardly know. And too expensive for me to accept since I hardly know you."

She smiled that smile and her eyes softened. "Forget about expense. Do you like it?" she asked. I had to admit I did. "It's exactly the kind of jewelry I would wear." Not too ostentatious and easily an everyday, practical piece.

"Well then, put it on," she said. I slipped it easily onto my right wrist as my left always wore a watch. "Well?" she waited for me to speak. A hundred thoughts burst from my carefully contained veneer protection. *"She must really like me. Today is a momentous day. Is she rich? I could get used to that. Maybe this is the beginning of something good. Oh, my. She likes me and I like her. What a great birthday!"*

"I love it. Thank you!" I moved closer to give her a warm thank you hug.

That eventful month and year was April, 2000. I have worn that bracelet almost every day since, only removing it to sleep or when showering or swimming.

Tuesday, September 11, 2001 was the day Ellie was scheduled to move into my house so we could live together. After the World Trade Center Towers were flown into and decimated that morning, the college I was teaching at closed and everyone was sent home. This was the same day the movers carried her items into my house. After each load, they stopped to watch the ongoing events every television station broadcasted. Ellie was at work, and they were not closing. We spoke on the telephone and she said she would be arriving late afternoon.

What was supposed to be a celebration of our next step in our relationship wasn't. Instead, we consoled each other and realized how thankful we were to be together and not in New York City when this horrendous event occurred.

I told her that even though it was awful, I was so glad to have her to witness it with.

As of the writing of this story, Ellie and I have been together twenty-one plus years.

We moved to Florida in 2002, and now summer in the upper peninsula of Michigan.

I did graduate to clipless peddles and a much lighter carbon fiber bicycle as time went on.

Ellie and I have bicycled from Boston to New York, New York to Boston, Boston to Provincetown, and Amsterdam to Paris in AIDS Rides to raise money and awareness for education and a cure for AIDS. We have hiked Mt. Washington in New Hampshire, traveled much of the US and Canada hiking and biking. The farthest we have traveled is South

Africa for a half Ironman triathlon and then a safari. Yes, Ellie became a triathlete, and I joke that the only vacations we take now are those that include a race. We also travel by RV because our rescue dog, Bailey Mama, is an integral part of our family and has to come with us, too.

We plan on staying active and healthy. Ellie has brought me immense happiness and healing. She has proven time and again how much she loves, likes, respects, and supports me. Meeting Ellie and continuing to live and love with her is the best of all things in my life. Having never thought I would find someone again, to having the best of the best, I am indeed a lucky and *still* smitten woman.

Timing Is Everything

He's a Keeper

by Rita Angelini

Couples today create a spectacle for their marriage proposals with the hope it goes viral. We didn't. After the church and reception hall were booked, Normann handed me a diamond engagement solitaire as an afterthought. Normann and I had dated for eight years, which included three breakups. When he thought of marriage as the next step in our relationship, his feet ran cold like glacier runoff. He got timid. A bit too timid, at times, but I ignored it.

I met him when I was a sophomore in college. I was looking forward to going out for dinner with my boyfriend at the time. Dressed and ready to go, I answered the ringing phone. He'd called to ask if we could spend our evening watching T.V. in his mother's living room, as we'd done for the past three months, so I slammed the phone on the hook, almost knocking it off the wall.

My older brother offered up a last-minute invitation to a Halloween party. I went. Marijuana and spilt beer permeated the smoky air, and one seedy man, with a skull attached to his fly zipper and a joint in his hand, approached me.

I ducked away and gravitated to the only other person who wasn't dressed in costume. Normann, at six-foot-two, with wiry blond hair, thick eyebrows, and a scraggly beard, was a plaid-wearing earthy guy. He asked who I was supposed to be.

I answered, "Depending on the circumstances, maybe a single lady."

Two months after we met, I was sure I wanted to keep Normann in my life. He showed me he was an honest man with a gentle heart, strong work ethic, and common sense. I was dating the bad boy who was on life's road to nowhere regardless of how much I prodded.

For our first date, he trimmed his beard and had his hair cut. I did a double take when I saw him. He was truly a diamond in the rough who only needed a woman's guidance in the grooming department. I hadn't realized his lack of vanity would result in constant reminders over the years to do it again and again.

Our second date, he called to ask if I'd had a chance to shop for Christmas.

I had recently been in a car accident that left me with two black eyes and a broken nose swollen to triple its normal size. "No, I'm staying inside until the swelling goes down."

"Nobody cares how you look. And if they do, it's their problem. Let them stare. I'm picking you up in forty-five minutes."

It amazed me that Normann didn't care how I looked, when my failing-at-saving-our-relationship, soon-to-be ex-boyfriend said he would see me after the bruising faded. I changed out of my sweats and T-shirt into snug-fitting jeans and a blouse for a trip to the mall. Under the harsh florescent lights, Normann said, "Your face is really beat up." He smiled. "You still look beautiful to me."

I smiled at that, as my ego needed a boost no matter how far-fetched. I planned an early evening because I had to work the next day, so I kept asking him what time it was. He noticed my constant need for the time and gave me a gold watch two days after Christmas.

This man was a keeper.

I invited him to share holidays with my family—he was sick, had to leave town unexpectedly; something suddenly came up. He attended my DePaul graduation ceremony and celebrated with me when I accepted my job offer from the largest accounting firm.

Then in June, on my twenty-first birthday before he was due to pick me up, he phoned. "I can't see you anymore."

"Excuse me? I don't think I heard you correctly." We hadn't had a fight. We hadn't even had one argument. I strained the phone cord as I raced into my brother's bedroom next to where the phone hung in the hall and slammed the door, the cord wedged in between the door and the jamb.

"I don't think we're right for each other."

"You're joking, right?"

"No." The line went dead.

I slid down the wall to the floor and kicked my brother's smelly socks and shoes away from me. With my knees scrunched to my chest, I dropped the phone on the rug. Tears rolled down my legs.

"You're going to break the cord," my dad yelled as he banged on the door.

I jumped up, swinging the door wide open. I slammed the phone on the hook and raced upstairs to my room. My father yelled again at my receding back.

It's his loss. It's his loss, I repeated to myself, when deep down it was my loss, too. Where was I going to find another guy my age that puts others before himself, offers to help before he's asked, and can fix things?

When I looked in my mirror, I saw a devastated girl. I wiped my tears and straightened my back. I don't need him.

Instead of sulking, I went to the neighborhood bar with my sisters and friends because we were regulars for ladies' night on Thursdays. We clinked our glasses to me, finally drinking legally. I sipped my cranberry-vodka, debating whether to obliterate my current memory with many more cocktails, though I had given up heavy drinking after my freshman year in college. Loud music pulsating, I struggled to hear a guy who talked to me on many occasions before. "Are you single? Do you want to go out with me?" he yelled.

I guess I am, I reasoned with myself. The best way to get over a broken heart was to find someone new. So we went on a couple dates. A rebound relationship, I compared everything he did to how Normann would have done, and he fell short. We lasted a few months before I called it off, blaming my new job as the reason.

In October, my sister begged me to call Normann, a mechanic, to look at her car with a stick-shift. She needed advice as to whether she should repair it or buy a new one. As she explained the problem, Normann's eyes strayed toward me. Several times he asked her to repeat what she said.

The few days after the first frost, a warm breeze rattled the leaves. Normann hunched under the hood. A leaf floated onto the engine. I leaned next to Normann, with his crazy blond hair standing erect, shouting for me to remind him about haircuts, to remove the leaf. Oil and gas emanated from the engine. We locked eyes, and I went a bit weak looking into his ocean blue irises.

Gone was the girl he left, hair tied up in a ponytail, wearing sweatpants who studied for four months straight to pass the CPA exam. Instead, I dressed in new white leather boots, acid washed jeans, and a flowing blouse, belted to show my twenty-six-inch waist. My thick auburn brown hair, layered, permed, and big on its own, didn't require teasing necessary in the 80s. My creamy flawless skin was accented with subtle hints of makeup, a detail I hadn't added to my face when I was with Normann.

His fingertips stained with grease, he pronounced her engine trashed. My sister and I planned to meet my fellow Arthur Andersen staff members downtown to watch the Bears football game. I thanked him and turned to wave goodbye again, satisfied with Normann's look of disbelief. I high-fived my sister once we were out of sight. I had funds, friends, and freedom. Eat your heart out Normann.

He called the next day. I was seeing several other men, but they fell to the wayside as Normann and I became exclusive. After two dates, I realized he planned to avoid the subject of our breakup.

My blunt nature sidestepped any tact––I asked, "Why did you break up with me?"

He stumbled over his tongue as he mumbled something about marriage and how I'd graduated.

"What does graduating have to do with marriage?"

"I thought you'd start hounding me about getting married because that's the next step."

"I don't know whose staircase you're going up, but no, it's not my next step. I don't want to get married. And what if I did? You just break up with me with no discussion? That's just wrong."

"I'm sorry. I lived through my parents' divorce, with them pitting me against the other, dishing out guilt trips because I wanted to see the other one. Holidays caused the biggest fights. When I was young, they fought about who got me when, and for how long, then they guilted me because I had a good time. I just don't think marriage is worth it. It's just a piece of paper."

After we were together for three more years, we talked about marriage. He spent nights at my condo and I spent nights at his house. We had several assets together, including a twenty-five-foot speedboat. It was the next step.

"I can't do this," he said when he called one Friday night. We'd planned to attend a neighborhood street fest with friends.

"We don't have to go. We can do something else," I said.

"I can't marry you." A click, and silence filled my ear.

In a fit of rage, I wanted to fling the cordless across the room, but if I broke it, I would be without a phone. Instead, I leashed my anger, shrugged, and shook my head with annoyance. I had traveled this road before.

I started dating someone else. Normann suggested as joint owners of the boat that we take a safety class to reduce our insurance rate. I took the bait, and by the end of the eight-week course, we were back together. After the first class, I asked why?

"Women changed when they get that ring on their finger. Nag. Nag. Nag. It's in all the movies. They don't have to be nice anymore. My friends' wives––they're bitchy. Look at your sisters. They're bossy and controlling. All because they have that piece of paper."

"I'm not an actor who can put on a show for five years. With me, what you see is what you get. As for my sisters, they were bossy and controlling before they got married."

A year later, we set an October wedding date, close to our seven-year anniversary of meeting. I picked out bridesmaid dresses and searched for the white satin dress of my dreams. We talked about kids. I didn't want nine like my mother, but from growing up in a large family, I wanted at least three. Apparently, that scared him, too.

He called again to end it. We loved each other. We trusted each other. How could he not see we were meant to be together? If he didn't have faith in our relationship, whether I wanted to or not, it was time for me to move on.

I piled his stereo, clothes, underwear, socks, and tooth-brush at the front door. When he came to my condo, frost oozed from my voice. "Think it over. This is the last time you're breaking up with me."

"I need more time."

I handed him the signed boat title.

This time, he was back two days later begging me to take him back. I resisted.

Three weeks later, we attended a musical-comedy, as we had purchased dinner-theater tickets months before.

Monday morning, he came to my work office bearing two dozen roses placed in Candlelight Playhouse commemorative glasses. The front desk called me to the lobby, so I walked to the far corner where he joined me.

He smiled and handed me the flowers. "I love you. I don't know why I'm being so weird about it. I don't want to live without you."

"Please go. Three times you've walked out on me. It won't happen a fourth," I hissed.

"We can fly to Vegas tonight and get it over with! Then it's done and I won't have to think about it anymore."

"Do you hear yourself?" I said in a hushed voiced. I turned to walk away, but he grabbed my arm.

"I love you."

I looked at his hand encircling my arm and, with a glare, told him to remove his hand from me.

In a halo of fragrance, I smiled at the receptionist as I walked past. "Lovely, aren't they?"

He left love notes on my car. I ignored them.

I was friendly with Normann, but our romance was over. I padlocked my heart no matter how much I wanted us to be together.

I met Dave and introduced him to my girlfriends, hoping he would date one of them. He said he enjoyed my company, and that was when I coordinated another group date. I planned to stay single. But the third date, I gave up. Dave and I started dating.

Dave offered to do the brakes on my car. He wasn't handy like you-know-who. I called Normann to fix Dave's repair job. Dave couldn't unclog my kitchen sink. He left as Normann came in with a plumbing rod, passing in the hall.

After six months of dating, Dave approached the subject of marriage. I could settle for Dave. He was kind, funny, and he liked to dance. If I opened my heart, I was sure I could find happiness with him and eventually come to love him as deeply as I had loved Normann. I probably could make it work.

But I realized I didn't want to be married unless I married Normann. He was my first real love. I loved him completely and unconditionally before knowing the pain of heartbreak. My head said no. He's hurt me too many times. My heart wanted to spend the rest of my life with Normann.

Once I admitted it to myself, I opened up to Normann.

We walked along the Chicago harbor shore where we had docked our boat in the summer. The harsh March winds blew, and I leaned into him, craving his warmth. This time he told me he feared having children, that our baby could have a disability—his sister had given birth to twins, one of whom died after two months from a brain injury at birth.

Normann said, "I want to spend the rest of my life with you. I can't guarantee we will have a large family."

"You don't have to guarantee anything."

He pulled my hands out of my pockets. "I don't have a ring, but I want to spend the rest of my life with you." He wrapped his warm hands around my cold fingers.

"I don't need a ring." We kissed.

We agreed not to set a number. One child at a time. If all went well, we'd consider having another. If things were rolling along, maybe another. Normann was always prepared for things to go wrong, while I remained an optimist. He was an extreme Boy Scout, making sure contingency plans were in place for possibilities. We balanced each other and butted heads.

We'd been together fifteen years, married almost six, when Marina, our first child, was born. Marina did what she was supposed to do—she ate, slept, and pooped. She hit the child development milestones on target. She was walking, babbling, and demanding in a flash. Two year later, we were ready to welcome another child.

And now we were living Normann's worst fear.

I gave birth to a robust, healthy, nine-pound baby girl, who nursed on schedule. But on the second day, KiKi stopped feeding and became agitated. Concerned with KiKi's crying, I questioned the nurse. The nurse brought KiKi to the nursery where she could observe her. She assured me my baby would resume nursing, but that didn't happen. A neonatologist examined her on the third day and explained that KiKi had contracted a bacterial infection. They transferred her to the neonatal intensive care unit. An antibiotic would eliminate the bacterial infection within three days. They sent us home without her.

At seven o'clock the next morning, the neonatologist called and informed us that KiKi had been placed into an induced coma. During the night, KiKi's heart had failed, said the voice on the phone, and for a period of time, her brain had been starved for oxygen. At the hospital they told us KiKi might not survive.

"Your daughter is going to need around-the-clock care for the rest of her life. She'll more than likely need to be institutionalized."

Normann rattled off questions. I didn't want to believe the doctors, though. I needed to see her, to hold her.

In the NICU, I stared at the tube down my baby's throat, the whirring ventilator linking her to life. There were no other parents in the room. The weight crashed down on me. and I collapsed alongside the incubator in a fetal position, awash in tears.Dizzy with fear.

Normann bent down and rubbed my back, and I felt his warm tears on my neck.

After thirty days in the neonatal intensive care unit, KiKi was finally discharged. They strongly encouraged institutional care and warned us KiKi probably would not walk or talk, would require a feeding tube, and her quality of life would benonexistent, thereby burdening our family. I thought about our two-year-old at home and if she would suffer.

I held my baby. "We can handle this," I said. The look on Normann's face suggested he was having second thoughts.

And he blamed me.

I felt the silent pressure building like water against a levee ready to collapse. His quiet anger was so great, I questioned whether our marriage would survive the first month after KiKi was born; he spoke to me only when necessary, while I wallowed in self guilt.

It was time to confront it. We would either drown in the deluge or learn to swim. Three days of KiKi's relentless crying, I was up during the night with her and up during the day with Marina. I napped when they both slept. My energy depleted——I refused to tolerate Normann's silent treatment any longer. We needed to voice our feelings so we could work to get past them.

I rocked KiKi in my arms as I speared a tasteless broccoli floret. As long as she had motion, she stayed quiet. "You need to talk to me."

He remained stoic. I imaged stabbing his hand with my fork to force a reaction. I tried again to initiate a conversation. He left the table, and I chased after him upstairs, KiKi weightless in my arms.

"You did this to our family." He erupted like a volcano oozing accusations and dire predictions of our destroyed family. "You changed from an obstetrician without discussing it with me! This is my baby, too. I should've had a say in the decision to change. And then you didn't even go to another doctor; you went to a midwife. A midwife! If you stayed with the doctor we wouldn't be in this situation."

I leaned toward him, finger pointing at air. "Midwives are qualified to deliver babies. I'm a healthy woman. It was supposed to be a simple delivery with no complications."

"Well, look where that got us."

"I wanted a better experience than what I had with Marina." A doctor had overdosed me with an epidural, finally showed up when I was fully dilated, and used forceps to deliver Marina. I didn't participate in the birth since I was unable to push. "Yes, Normann, I should've talked to you before I changed. That's water under the bridge."

"Your sisters knew about you changing practices and had input in your decision. Where was I in the decision? I didn't learn about it until after you changed."

"They used midwives to deliver their babies. They had personal experience. Of course I was going to get their input."

"And then you had to change again because they fired all the midwives."

"They didn't fire the midwives. That group decided not to use midwives anymore."

"I wonder why."

"There's a difference between getting fired for incompetence and being let go because of how a doctor conducts his practice."

"So where did that lead you? To someone you had no idea about. We saw how competent she was. You're going to have to live with your decision. And now, Marina, KiKi, and I have to live with the results of that decision, too. It's going to take me some time to get over this. Right now, I'm pissed." The midwife had used a medically accepted protocol at the time that didn't detect an infection present which had caused KiKi's illness and subsequent brain damage.

Two days later, when I found the time to brush my teeth, I saw our toothbrushes hugging, the bristles intertwined. Normann put them together as a sign we would survive this together.

KiKi's life tested our limits—illnesses, hospitalizations, excessive crying, and her lack of childhood development. What came naturally for Marina, KiKi had therapists trying to teach her how to roll, to reach, to sit, to swallow, and to talk, without success. Before Marina could talk, she could point, grab, or stomp to get what she needed. I deciphered KiKi's cries with fifty-fifty accuracy.

Marina showed her frustration with KiKi's constant wailing, innocently kissing KiKi's toe then biting it, or getting KiKi a toy and telling her to "catch it" while flinging it at KiKi's head. Medical equipment, a Little Tykes Kitchen, and toy bins replaced the coffee table, floor planters, and a recliner. In KiKi's quieter, healthier moments, Marina dragged her by the foot inside the soft cottony blanket-fort built over the dining room table. Marina pretend-fed KiKi plastic food and placed a doll next to her so she could play, too. Deep in her throat, KiKi voiced her aahs. Other times Marina played a game with KiKi, jumping over her, and if KiKi's random swinging arm touched Marina, KiKi won. KiKi gurgled her delight.

Normann played with Marina, and baby KiKi watched. As Normann learned to care for KiKi he realized she wasn't as fragile as he thought. Now she wrestled, got tossed and tickled by Normann just like her big sister. He no longer feared he would break her. KiKi arched with joy as Normann entered the back door from work. Marina raced to hug him, and he swung her up in the air. KiKi's face beamed with excitement as she anticipated her turn. Normann dumped Marina headfirst onto the loveseat and she giggled. He then turned his attention to KiKi.

"Whose belly am I going to eat? I'm hungry." He smacked his lips.

KiKi's legs thrashed. He blew loud raspberries on her stomach and grabbed her foot to munch on. Her arms flung with pleasure.

Marina sat on Normann. As a bucking bronco, he reared, and Marina held onto his neck. "KiKi's turn," Marina said. I held KiKi on Normann's back as he crawled and arched his back. KiKi giggled.

We came to an acceptance, this was our life, and put our daughters as our priority. I carved out "Marina time" when we went to park or out for ice cream without KiKi. We searched for alternative therapies that would help KiKi with basic skills—rolling, sitting, crawling, or walking—locally, throughout the US, and internationally. Traditional therapy at home didn't help her reach any milestones.

When KiKi was three and Marina was five, the whole family traveled to Poland so KiKi could participate in a grueling, month-long, intensive physical therapy program, six days a week, five hours a day. We continued the program for many years and KiKi developed enough upper body strength to push a walker and take steps. This program gave us hope that KiKi would someday walk.

On our first free day, Normann pushed KiKi's wheelchair up the steep ramp, steps filled in with concrete on the edge of the crumbling stairs. The Baltic Sea air was biting; puddles almost iced over. Leaves rustled on the ground as the wind gusted. We looked for a place to shop and warm up after the bus ride. People spoke what sounded to like gibberish as they hurried by.

Signs strung endless consonants with few vowels in store fronts with tiny handwritten translations in English below. A jewelry store was open, and we went in mainly to get out of the wind. Marina traveled from display case to display case filled with amber necklaces and rings, leaving smudges on the glass in her wake. A small display section glittered with gold and diamonds. One caught my eye, a simple gold band paved with tiny gems.

I didn't need it. I didn't even wear my diamond engagement ring. On my left ring finger, I wore the thin gold band he slipped on my finger twelve years ago.

Normann followed my gaze. "Do you want it?"

I'd learned to give up a lot since KiKi was born. "I don't need it." Trinkets and figurines had lost their appeal, more things to dust and keep track of.

"I didn't ask if you needed it. I asked if you wanted it."

I imagined the ring beside my wedding band. "Only if you're telling me you'd marry me all over again."

Normann gestured to the man which ring I'd like to see. It sparkled in my hand. Marina wanted to see. I showed KiKi, and she gurgled. I tried it on and it fit. Normann bought the ring and we went outside.

The clouds opened up and a few stray rays of sun peeked down. Normann bent down on one knee and slipped the diamond band on my finger. "I would marry you all over again, even knowing what was to come." He gazed into my eyes and whispered, "I love you."

I gasped as my hands flew to my cheeks—this was better than his first proposal, when he'd handed me a diamond ring in my kitchen and asked, "Do you want it?"

He worried about our future before we were married, and decided at that moment our crazy present life was worth doing again.

To this day, I wear the diamond band bought in Poland first, which represents his direct connection to my heart, and then my gold band he slipped on my finger thirty years ago.

Yes, this man is definitely a keeper.

A Diamond Is Forever

by Chelsea Fuchs

Everyone remembers their engagement story. It's written with indelible ink on your heart. Each moment seared into your brain so you can revisit the day from time to time. I'm no different.

Yet, my first engagement was not my last. The first time, I was on a school bus on the way to the zoo. And I was five. We were on a kindergarten field trip, he'd had no ring, and I said yes anyway. Then he moved away two years later, and I never saw him again.

The second proposal happened in first grade. There was a ring this time, but since my heart already belonged to another adorable boy, I tried to let my admirer down as easily as I could. After all, marriage was an important thing, and I didn't think I could be engaged to two boys at the same time.

Proposal number three was from a salesman who was joking because I was so amazing and knew so much about the computer he was trying to sell my parents. He back-pedaled quickly when I told him I was only thirteen.

When I turned eighteen and had still had never had a boyfriend, I told myself I was okay with being single.

Up until that point, I didn't see the use of wasting time with boys who were just going to break my heart. I wanted to find my soulmate, and I refused to settle for anything less. I was a bit of a handful, unapologetically, and on purpose.

If I pushed a boy too far and they went away, then clearly, they weren't man enough for me and my high expectations as to what a relationship was truly meant to be. I wanted nothing less than a love that lasted until the end of time.

I was a flirt and a tease, but I wasn't easy. I felt safe acting that way because I refused to have a boyfriend and knew it wouldn't go beyond a harmless flirtation. I wasn't allowed to date until I was sixteen, and the good girl I was, I wanted to honor my parents' wishes. That didn't stop the offers from the boys that flirted back and then asked me out.

I was flattered by the attention, but they would inevitably run away when I bared my claws and acted less than cute or cuddly. My mom called my sister and I her kittens when we were little. My favorite shirt, from Hot Topic, was one with a definition:

Kitten (n): cute, cuddly, with claws.

That tee fit me to a tee.

Love is funny, though. When I was ten, I developed a crush on one particular boy. I liked him for seven years. A part of me will always think of that crush fondly. But I didn't marry him.

Love is so funny that I married the boy I didn't like for four years and then was crazy about for the three years we started dating.

The boy I liked was safe and didn't make me cry. But we never ended up together. It wasn't meant to be.

Yet, the boy I married broke my heart before we were ever together.

I gave him a ride home when we were fourteen.

I painted his toenails when we were fifteen.

He made me cry at sixteen.

He tried to be my secret admirer at seventeen.

And I eventually told him I loved him at eighteen.

At nineteen, I reminded him I wouldn't marry him until we were at least twenty-one.

He proposed at twenty.

We wed at twenty-one.

Like most of our story, it's not a straight line from beginning to end. It twisted and turned, folding in on itself and straightening out to reach the ending. It all started, at least for me, on a band trip to Dallas, Texas.

We were freshman, and Brandon and I had become friends. Not super close quite yet, but this boy in his red flannel jacket was kind and friendly—and completely scary.

He had a smile, but he rarely used it. He was serious when everyone else was being silly. He knew where he wanted to go in life.

As part of the trip, we went to the Galleria, a mall in Dallas. A group of us wandered from store to store. We went inside an electronics store and settled down into the comfy seats in front of the too-big-for-life TVs. We all daydreamed about our futures.

"I want to be rich—" I began.

My friend, Jake, cut me off. "And famous, yeah, yeah."

I shook my head. "No. Just rich, not famous."

"And what will you do when you're rich but not famous?" Paul, the resident jokester, asked.

"You'll tell me jokes," I said as I pointed to Paul. "And not let the money go to my head." Turning to Jake, I continued, "You will design my house's sound system." Since he was the one that was explaining how cool the system was in front of us.

"And you will teach me to play the trombone," I said to Joseph. We'd had several classes together since we started high school, and all became good friends.

"What about Brandon?" Paul asked. Brandon sat behind me, out of my line of sight.

"Brandon?" My heart fluttered. How could I have forgotten Brandon? "Well, he'll be my bodyguard and make sure I'm happy." I nodded my head. That made sense. Someone should always oversee my happiness. I'm not even sure why I said it, but his "job" seemed the best fit of all the ones I listed. I thought it was a great idea, but he didn't smile. One side of his mouth twitched, but that was all.

With that funny feeling sticking around in my chest, I jumped up. "I think it's time to get back to the busses. Let's make like a banana and blow this popsicle stand."

And so it began, my bodyguard and happiness coordinator was never far away, keeping me well-entertained. We grew closer over the months. Little by little, he broke down my walls, becoming my best friend. The hours we spent on the phone were often consumed by my throwing out random questions, just to see if I could stump him. He always played along, and I often laughed at what crazy ideas we'd come up with.

The next year, our sophomore year, Brandon drove me home from Solo and Ensemble, another band competition. Brandon was so engaged in what he was saying, he ran a stop sign while talking to me.

"Did you just go through that stop sign?" I asked and laughed at his flustered expression.

"Which stop sign?" He looked around the street in confusion. I craned my head out the window to see the name of the street he'd just flown past.

"Alice," I laughed. The street's name was Alice. "If we ever have kids, we should name our daughter, Alice."

"Alice would be a weird name for a boy." He continued to drive down the street.

I crossed my arms. "Who said anything about having a boy?"

"You're the one saying we're going to have kids. I'm going to become an F-15 fighter pilot. I won't have time to have kids. I'm going to be a Blue Angel."

"Oh, come on, play the game. If it's a boy, then, what would you name him?" I asked. Brandon was very used to my games of 'what if' or 'would you rather.'

"I guess the next road sign I roll through," he reasoned.

"But what if it's Pennsylvania or some other awful name?" I asked, trying to hold back my giggles.

"Anything would be better than Alice for a boy," he reasoned.

Time passed, like it always does, and another year rolled by, accompanied by a new flannel jacket. Shortly before The Big Fight, someone asked me why I didn't just put Brandon out of his misery and be his girlfriend already.

"If I went out with him," I said and looked at him from across the band room. "I'd have to marry him. And I'm not ready for that type of commitment."

"Good grief, Chelsea. It's a date, not a marriage proposal."

But to me, it was one in the same. I refused to date a boy I wasn't willing to marry. And I wasn't ready to marry Brandon, yet. I had too much to do, like conquer the world first. I knew a serious relationship with Brandon would change everything.

Silly teenagers do silly things, and so for months, Brandon and I didn't speak. The Big Fight was the worst time of my life. For a time after that, any interaction between us was painful. But he had made promises, the least of which was that he'd marry me if neither of us were married by our fifteenth high school reunion. I wasn't sure how that would work out since we still couldn't be near each other without me feeling the need to cry.

As the days of high school came to a close and our time together seemed to be slipping away, something changed. I realized I needed him to be in my life. A dream and a drive changed that, and now here we were, boyfriend and girlfriend. I'd never been anyone's girlfriend before, but I knew that I liked him.

No. "Like" was too simple of a word. I loved him. The serious boy in the flannel jacket.

As fate would have it, three months into my first ever relationship, it was time for me to go away to college—to a school where the boys outnumbered the girls, three to one. Brandon stayed and started his culinary arts degree.

As it turned out, dating your best friend can be hazardous to his health and bank account.

During our first semester of college, Brandon made the hour and a half trip from his house to Socorro to see me every Tuesday, before turning around and driving home that night. After a semester of spending over a thousand dollars on gas, his focus went from keeping his girlfriend away from the plethora of males to getting his school transfer accepted. Deciding that another thousand dollars' worth of gas probably wasn't the best idea, he left his flannel jacket behind so I wouldn't get cold, and we decided to see each other only on the weekends.

Wearing his jacket was the next best thing to having him there with me. The time previously spent on the road was now spent on studying. After a year and a half of a

long-distance relationship, Brandon finally started his education at the same college, and he almost smiled at that.

The Christmas break before he started at Tech, my great
grandma passed away. She was ninety-one years old and
had lived to see a great-great granddaughter—my cousin's
daughter had been born just days before my grandma's final
hospitalization. Brandon asked if he needed to come to the
funeral two states away. I told him it was okay to miss. He
had to pack for the dorm anyway.

"How was the funeral?" he asked when we'd gotten
back home.

"It was okay," I replied. "Look what my great aunt gave
me." I showed him a diamond pendant. My sister received a
similar necklace to remember our great grandma by. "When
you go to buy my engagement ring, you can use this diamond if you like." The thought of having a family heirloom
as part of our love story made me happy.

Our first semester at the same college passed quickly. It
was tremendous seeing Brandon every day, and both our
grades improved, staying at school over the weekends and
studying together rather than spending every night talking
on the phone. With Brandon's cooking experience, he found
a job at the best restaurant in Socorro. Soon it was summer
and time for my cousins' weddings.

It was the morning of my cousin's wedding, and we were
driving down to Las Cruces, New Mexico to attend the ceremony. I'd gone over to Brandon's student apartment to wait
for my parents. He had air-conditioning, and the swamp
cooler in my off-campus house wasn't keeping up with the
100+ temperatures. Evaporative cooling cools, but only so
much. While I waited in his room, I heard him gagging in

the shower. In the two years we'd been together, Brandon had never gotten sick.

«Are you okay?» I yelled out.

"Yeah," he called back. "Just choked myself on my toothbrush."

I nodded my head. I have a horrible gag reflex, so that happens to me all the time.

On the way out the door, Brandon asked if he could ride with my dad. As I tried to hop in the Jeep, I was rudely interrupted.

"Yeah, I meant, could I ride with your dad alone."

I shrugged. Before Brandon came down to Tech, he and my dad used to play racquetball a couple times a week together. They'd become good friends during the time we'd been dating, and I assumed he must have been missing my dad. I got in the other car with my mom and sister, happy for the girl time.

The wedding was a long, Catholic affair. What I loved most was seeing two people start their lives together. I glanced at Brandon during the ceremony often, wondering when he was going to get around to asking me to marry him. I told him I didn't want to get married until we were old enough to legally participate in the champagne toast, but doubt was beginning to creep in. That was only a year away and we'd been together for two years. We had many talks about our future together. Wasn't it about time to start planning?

A few weeks later, my family attended another wedding for a different cousin. This time, Brandon wasn't able to come with us. He was prepping for finals and pulling more shifts than usual at work, so he couldn't spend the weekend with me.

The wedding was near my grandparents' home, and my parents and I were staying there that weekend. Brandon had become a vital part of working the cattle every spring and fall, and my Grandma Jeanne had recently stopped making cookies with nuts because she'd overheard Brandon and I squabbling about his dislike of nuts. I was of the firm believe that nuts made everything better, while he disagreed.

"I can't believe she took the nuts out for him," I muttered as I sat alone at my grandma's kitchen table, eating a cookie and missing both the pecans and that hairy-legged boy, as my dad referred to him. I wondered why he was picking up so many extra shifts at the Brew Pub, the nickname for the local brewery and wood oven pizza place where he cooked. Was he tired of me and my family? He'd never said no to a trip to Cliff before now. Did weddings make him nervous? I thought we had the same vision for our future. We'd gone and looked at a few rings, so I thought he was ready to propose. We'd talked about my life plan. Getting married at twenty-one, finishing school, having kids, someday buying a ranch of our own.

Did he not want to spend forever with me?

There is a certain romance in being a poor, starving college student. Our needs are less, but everything costs more than the money that you have. Summer quickly came to an end, and so did the normal craziness of balancing the school year with the part time jobs we had started again. I somehow managed to pass Calc. III on the first try over the summer, which was a huge improvement over my multiple tries through Calc. I and Calc. II. I was praying I'd have the same success with Differential Equations. Not driving home every weekend to see Brandon helped my grades, and being in the same town as me helped his savings account.

Like most nights when he wasn't working, Brandon was at my house studying. My roommate patiently helped him with his Calc. I homework while she and I worked through our Differential Equation homework. She was taking the class as well, and she was the only reason I had any hope of passing the class.

Chemistry, not math, was my strong suit. Brandon had to finish his Calc. Homework, and then we were going to review for his chemistry test the next day. As we snuggled on the floor next to my bed, something continued to poke me in the side.

"What's in your pocket?" I asked and tried to move it out of the way. The offending object didn't move. Poking and prodding at it, it was solid and felt like a box. "Why do you have a box in your pocket?"

A lightbulb went off in my head. Maybe we were on the same page after all. "Is that my engagement ring?"

"No," Brandon replied and closed his chemistry book.

"If it was and you wanted to see if it would fit, I'd close my eyes," I reasoned as my pulse picked up speed and I extended my hand.

"It's not your engagement ring."

"Oh," I said, crestfallen. I tried not to let my emotions taint my voice. If it wasn't my engagement ring, then why wouldn't he tell me what was in his pocket? He never kept things from me. Were we drifting apart?

"Let's get back to studying, then."

We continued to review his chemistry until David Letterman came on.

"I'll stay for the Top Ten list and then I've got to get home," Brandon said. We settled in to watch.

"Aren't you going to go get some water?" Brandon asked.

"No, I'm not thirsty," I replied. I'd really hoped he was going to propose tonight. It was the thirteenth, and I loved that number. Brandon knew it too.

The Top Ten list that night was from the national competition for the mating call of some exotic bird.

I turned off the TV. Brandon rolled off the couch and onto his knee.

"What are you doing?" I asked and stood up. My pulse rate went through the roof. Was this happening? Was he proposing or was this another false start?

"I've been trying to do this all day, but you kept ruining my plans. So here it is." He pulled out the box from his pocket. It was blue and silver and had the name of the nicest jewelry store in Albuquerque on it. He lifted the box up and cracked it open.

"I knew it!" I squealed.

"Are you going to let me propose now?" he asked. "I do have to get some sleep tonight so I can take that chemistry test tomorrow."

I nodded my head, yes. My heart overflowed with excitement and joy.

"I love you, Chelsea. I always have. I knew on the first day of band camp freshman year, when I saw you on the twenty-yard line, that you were it for me. I wanted to marry you then. Will you marry me?" Brandon asked, a smile trying to peak around his stern expression.

The boy that rarely smiled was almost smiling.

I nodded my head yes but then stopped. "Wait. Did you—"

"Yes, I asked your dad for permission," Brandon said, knowing me so well. "On the way to the wedding in July. That's why I was throwing up that day. You're the one with the awful gag reflex, not me."

I laughed as I nodded my head yes.

He slipped the ring on my finger. There were two smaller diamonds on either side of a slightly bigger one in the middle, set in white gold.

"That middle diamond was from your necklace. Your mom gave it to me after I asked your dad for permission. I couldn't go with you to the wedding last month because I was pulling double shifts so I could pick up the ring before we went branding cattle, but it got held up."

"We've got to call our parents," I cheered as my roommate came out of her room. "Look," I said as I held up my hand. "Brandon proposed!"

Six years might have passed since I first noticed the boy in the flannel jacket who had a smile but didn't use it often. The jackets had changed in pattern, but the boy hadn't. He spent the rest of the evening smiling.

Epilogue- Sixteen years later

"What do you want for our fifteenth anniversary?" Brandon asked as we drove down the same highway where our relationship had started that one fateful June day, so many years ago. I fussed with his green flannel jacket, covering my legs, rather than turning up the heater. I was always cold, and he was always hot, and I'd learned how to best manage the heater so we were both comfortable, which usually involved me bringing extra jackets.

"I think I'd like some bigger diamond earrings," I said and played with the little diamond studs my parents had given me on my sixteenth birthday.

"Oh?" he asked. I'm not a big jewelry person, and while he'd given me pearls for our first married Christmas, I'd never asked for jewelry before.

"I think it would be wonderful to give each of the kids one of the earrings for when they get engaged. They could have it mounted in their own rings or trade it in for something else. Having that diamond from my grandma was such a blessing, I'd like to continue on the tradition."

And so, some day, when our children find their others, they'll each have a part of our love story to start their new lives together.

On Top of the World

by Renee Adamowicz-Schwartz

Chuck and I met through work. We both worked for different technology companies. There was an immediate synergy between the two companies, and they began talking about a merger. That is when we first met. After the merger we were asked to attend a conference together. I would say this is where the real Chuck and Renee met. It was going to be a long travel day, and we had never really met before, only once before at a meeting when the companies discussed the merger. It appeared that Chuck was someone that enjoyed talking, and he was a good communicator (I noticed that right away) this was not something I was used with the guys I hung out with. He seemed to care for others, he listened to me when I talked (really listened, it was almost awkward – I guess I got used to people just yessing me). He wanted to get to know me and he wanted to discuss his life with me. He encouraged conversation – he was smart, funny, and most of all seemed to be true, and in return I was able to be me, and be honest and true. He was thoughtful and he asked if I needed a break or something to eat. *Wow,* I thought to myself, *most men I knew would do anything not to stop on a road trip.* Looking back now this really was the start of a great connection. We had a long drive back and forth to that conference and it was there we laid it all out – we made a friendship.

When we returned from the conference and went to work together in the same office for the first time, I saw a different Chuck. One I really didn't know. He wasn't really the same person that I met on the trip, he was more reserved, serious, and stern. At that moment I said to myself – *I have met the real Chuck, and I will now meet some other Chuck* (who knows, maybe he felt the same about me). That was okay, there were no heartfelt, emotional feelings there – it was all good. We both accepted it without words. One thing that did remain was that we were buddies, like two guy friends or two girlfriends – we complemented each other and there were times the real Chuck and Renee would come out, and we would laugh and joke. Over this time, we worked together for over nine years – we became the Chuck and Renee Show to many. The staff got used to us bickering, and the clients loved the way we worked together for them. We were an awesome work team. We worked hard together, we both stood strong for our own goals – we defended our own thoughts and the goals of our clients! It was really a great team. It was never a thought of anything beyond that. We knew we got to meet the real Chuck and Renee the first time we met (no trying to be someone else to impress the other person, no tip toeing around the other person) and that was comfortable for the both of us. One day, something magical happened, and the timing was right. Call it the right place and the right time, I am not sure how to describe it, but that long friendship started to blossom into something more. We began to date, and it was an easy transition from being friends to wanting to become intimate for the both of us.

As we progressed in our relationship, about three to four years in, we began talking about marriage and getting engaged. Once those talks were underway, I started to get a twinge of excitement, and I let out a big smile.

Once the excitement wave passed, the in-charge Renee took over (she is never too far). I am someone who knows what I want. So, once the subject came up about getting engaged, I began searching for my perfect ring. When it came time to think of the diamond, I knew I wanted it to be different, to be special (I am not a very traditional person). It didn't take long for me to decide. My favorite color is yellow; it reminds me of bright and sunny days. It was then I decided I wanted a yellow diamond. I was not sure about the shape, size, or setting, but when I saw it, I would know.

I did a lot of random searching online. One day, there it was, a yellow diamond in the perfect woven setting that had shiny little diamonds around it. Its name was Sunny Days, a nickname I got from when I was younger. I used to wake up in the morning and say, "Morning sunshine!" I loved yellow, I was always happy, bubbly, and out for a good time. Some people started to call me sunshine. I named my bowling ball sunshine, and when I was able to buy my gently used 2004 BMW convertible, I purchased vanity plates (which I didn't imagine I would ever do) and I named my BMW with those plates, SUNEDAZ. *It's perfect,* I thought. But how could I be sure? I would have to live with it for the rest of my life. I needed to see it in person.

I told Chuck, "I think I found the ring." I showed him what it looked like.

He said, "It's perfect, it's you! I'll buy it."

"No, we need to see it in person."

He agreed.

As I researched more, I learned the setting was made by a designer in California, and it was only sold in very limited locations. I found a private jeweler in New York City and gave the information to Chuck.

Chuck made all the arrangements. He called the jeweler and made an appointment for us, she agreed to have the ring on site for us to see it. Chuck scheduled the day: a train ride into NYC and a nice dinner out. This was something I appreciated about Chuck from the time I met him, he is very thoughtful in all he does. When we arrived, we were standing outside a building – not a jewelry store. We looked at each other and then went over to the building to see if her name was on it. Yes, it was. We pressed the button and told her who we were, and she buzzed us up. It was a small, private office/showroom – it was intimate and exciting. We trusted her since the designer of the ring was reputable and we didn't imagine them aligning with someone that would not work with the upmost integrity. She sat us down, offered us some water and then took out a soft felt cloth and laid the ring on it. From the moment we saw the ring, I immediately fell in love with it —its sparkle, its elegance, it was perfect.

Chuck turned to me and said, "Now it's up to me. You won't know where, when, or how I will ask you. It could be two days, two months, two years. I got this, trust me."

So, I did just that. I put it out of my head.

Well, that was until we planned a trip to Paris.

I remembered that beautiful ring and how nice it would be to finally have it on my finger, sparkling my way through the days and nights until I get married. Knowing how thoughtful and romantic Chuck could be, I thought, *This is it! I am going to live the dream of so many others out there and get engaged in Paris.*

We had many things planned, but the highlight would be a gourmet pairing wine lunch in the Eiffel Tower. I knew this had to be it, a thought that would be hard to resist even for a gal like me. I hadn't planned this day all my life—no picture books, magazines, well thought out plans or expectations. I never thought of myself as someone that would ever get married. But once I met Chuck and spent time with him, I realized what a true relationship was, what trust and love were. I knew I was ready.

We were at the top of the world and had just enjoyed an unbelievable seven courses and wine tasting menu at the restaurant in the Eiffel Tower. We had different waiters for each course, we had a sommelier in person (a sommelier is formally trained in and specializes in all aspects of wine service, wine and food pairings, and wine storage). In this case, he tasted every bottle of wine that was opened for us and approved it before it would be served. This was something I had never experienced before. We were just in awe. Each dish was beautifully presented. When it came to dessert it was a work of art, we had three courses of desserts. I remember at one point heading to the ladies' room and just looking around the at the whole restaurant, which was glass, and you could see the views of Paris from all directions. At that moment I said to myself, *am I really here? This is like a dream, and to think, soon I will be engaged.* It was the most delightful experience, and it made me feel like a queen.

Then we made our way to the top of the Eiffel Tower. I felt nervous and excited at the same time. The elevator stopped and we got off.

It was a clear, beautiful day, and the views were spectacular. From where we were standing, we were about 984 feet up. You could see a panoramic view of the city, the buildings, the lay of the land, and the park below. It seemed like you could see forever. People were all about, and all I could think of was the moment he would ask me to marry him. *How will he do it? What will he say?* As we strolled the top and took in the vibes of love all around us, we walked by a man selling champagne.

I said, "We should buy some champagne."

Chuck graciously said, "We had so much wine with lunch, I don't want to spoil that adventure we just had."

I calm down inside and say to myself, *Let him do it his way. After all, I am going to get engaged on the top of the Eiffel Tower in Paris. What more can you ask for?*

So, we looked at the views, took some pictures, snuck in some kisses, and then went to the elevator—

Wait, what?

Before I knew it, we stepped inside. The elevator started going down. How could this be? He forgot to ask me to marry him. We don't have any other plans to come back here. I feel like my heart just fell 984 feet to the ground – maybe even crushed, crushed like the grapes in the champagne we didn't get to try. Does he know what he has just done? This is every girl's dream, well, almost everyone's, and now it even became mine. The event of a lifetime gone in one push of an elevator button.

I knew I had to bounce back; I didn't want to ruin the trip over this missed opportunity of a lifetime. I tried not to think about it. I realized I had to let it go and that it would happen when it would happen. Chuck was in control, and I had to let that be. We continued our trip and took in more sights, dinners, and romantic moments, but no engagement. I really didn't expect it to happen any other way, so I didn't have any other expectations as the trip went on.

Before I knew it, the trip was over, and we were on the plane back home and decidedly not engaged. At that moment I said to myself, *That's it. I give up. I will never anticipate this moment again.* That was in October of 2013.

On December 31, 2013, Chuck arranged for us to have a date night and celebrate New Year's Eve. Date night was something we did every few months.

"Let's do it in style," he said. "Just me and you this New Year's."

Usually, we would spend the holiday with family or friends, but it had been a while since we had a great night out alone together, so it made sense.

I jumped at the invite. "Let's do it!"

We loved getting dressed up and going to a hotel—checking into our room, hanging out at the lobby bar, chatting it up with people, having dinner, drinks, and going back to our room. It was a tradition we started when we first got together, so I really didn't think anything of it.

As we planned for our New Year's date night, I wondered what I should wear. I was trying to think of what the hotel had planned—maybe a grand party. Now that would be fun!

"Don't pack anything too fancy," Chuck said. "We are going to be a little casual on this trip."

"Really, what do you think I should pack?"

"Maybe a nice top, slacks, and comfortable shoes. I have something planned for us."

I made a bit of a face but went along with it. I trusted him, and he had been learning from me how to be spontaneous and adventurous, so I left it up to him.

Just days later, the time had come and we were on our way to the hotel. When we arrived, he said, "Let's get checked in and dressed. After that, we can go to the lobby bar for a drink and wait for the car to pick us up."

"The car?" I asked.

"It's New Year's Eve and I really don't want to be out there drinking and driving so I arranged for a car to pick us up."

"Where are we going? I thought we were staying here."

Chuck said, "It's a surprise, an adventure as you like to say."

"I'm just going with the flow." I am sticking to my vow not to anticipate a thing anymore after that disastrous let down in Paris.

When the car arrived, Chuck whispered to the driver, "Do not mention where we are going. Please just get us there." I was curious, excited, and enjoying the moment. I didn't know where we were going, and I was loving it.

We climbed in and off we went. I didn't know what to expect or how long this ride would be. About fifteen minutes later, we arrived. I could see the sign as big as the sunrise, bright and bold. Dave & Busters.

I burst out laughing.

This happened to be one of the first dates Chuck and I ever went on. Dave & Busters had state-of-the-art games, food, bar, and TVs, and you could walk around with your drinks and play the games. It was like an adult arcade, and I was looking forward to another fun date (and kicking Chuck's butt in air hockey).

"Are you happy?" he asked. "Do you like it? They had a catering package so we will have dinner, music, and get to play games all night and celebrate New Year's together."

Was I happy? I was ecstatic. "This is an awesome plan!"

As we made our way to the party room, Chuck said, "They are also doing a giveaway to a tropical island right before midnight and we are entered."

"I'm so excited. I love raffles and giveaways." Of course, what I really love is winning them.

As we entered, there were others who also signed up for the package, all adults having fun. The room was fully decorated—the tables had balloons, party favors, and bottles of champagne for a midnight toast. They had an open bar and a buffet of different appetizers and foods. It really was a great way to spend New Year's Eve. I was impressed with Chuck's plan. I quickly grabbed a sparkly crown and some beads for Chuck, and off we went into the playroom. We had wrist bands that allowed us to play anything and everything as many times as we liked. We drank, we ate, we played tons of games—some single games and some competitive (I won those of course), and most of all we hugged, kissed, and laughed. We met and chatted with others; it was perfect. Little did I know how perfect it really was.

We were done playing and ready to settle down to bring in the New Year. They brought out desserts and made sure we all had nice glasses of champagne for our toast. As it got closer to midnight, the excitement built, and people were putting on party hats, crowns, beads, and having fun with the noise makers. The time got even closer, and a little before midnight the music stopped, and the DJ announced he was going to be giving away a trip to the Caribbean. *Oh, I can't wait, I love to win!*

A drum roll echoed through the room. The DJ announced, "And the winner is... Renee Adamowicz."

I jumped up and said, "That's me! That's me!" I screamed at the top of my lungs. I looked to Chuck. "I won! I won!" A huge smile stretched across his face. I ran up to the stage to get my prize. The DJ congratulated me and handed me three envelopes and a bottle of champagne.

I grabbed them and turned around to everyone cheering. I made my way back to my seat, waving my prizes in the air. I assumed the envelopes were information about the trip. As I walked back, I looked down and noticed they were hand-written. The handwriting looked familiar.

Envelope #1 said, *Open me first,* #2 said, *Open me second,* #3 said, *Open me last.* I began to open the first and the DJ played a song in the background, one very special to me. Chuck would always sing James Taylor, the song about how she moves. As I opened the envelope and heard the song, tears streamed down my face. I was built up with so much emotion and not even sure why. I was there in the moment as if I were alone.

I sat down and took out the note and began reading it. Some of the words from the James Taylor song playing in the background were on it, and on the bottom, it said, *Open #2 now.*

These notes were full of thoughtful words of love, romantic rhythms, and quirky little things that have great meaning to me and Chuck. When I got to the bottom of letter #3 it said, *Open the box next.*

Box?

I looked up and Chuck was on his knee holding a small box. A woman behind me yelled, "She's getting engaged!"

It was as if I woke up from a trance. As I looked through my tears, Chuck knelt in front of me with the ring—our ring, the most perfect ring—smiling and waiting to ask me to marry him officially with his words. He looked into my eyes and said, "Baby, I love you, will you marry me?"

I wrapped my arms around him and hugged him like never before. "Yes! Yes! Yes!"

I couldn't believe it. A rush came over me. I knew I was really on top of the world this time. Paris had nothing on this most thoughtful, playful, perfect, beautiful moment. Chuck did it. He made this an event I would never forget or ever want to replace.

We hugged and kissed, and moments later, the clock struck midnight. We enjoyed our champagne toast and all the people wishing us love and happiness. At last, there we were, heading into the New Year happily engaged.

Even to the sweet end, Chuck had given thought to every detail. In the past when we discussed getting married, we brought up the Caribbean—an intimate wedding with close family and friends and a great vacation. Chuck was so thoughtful like that. I may be adventurous, but boy, can he make a well thought-out plan.

I had to tell Chuck about my thoughts on Paris. "Did you ever intend for that to be the place where you'd ask me to get married?"

"I knew you were disappointed. I could tell by your face," he said, "I purposely didn't bring the ring to Paris because I knew I couldn't control myself there." Paris will do that to you.

We laughed as I told him about all the things that were going through my head, and how in the end I had to give in, and I left it all up to him.

"I wanted to wait for the right moment, something not cliche."

Boy, am I ever glad he didn't bring that ring to Paris. The whole plan of getting us together where we had our first date was the beginning of such thoughtful and well thought out events that lead to our engagement, down to the raffle for a trip to the Caribbean – where we would eventually marry. I knew when I first me Chuck he was a thoughtful, kind, loving person and he had lived up to that and beyond and I am so honored to have him as my husband. Forever more, Dave & Busters will always be the most romantic place in the world to me. I am eternally grateful that our two companies merged. I believe that somewhere, somehow, the universe knew we needed to meet, and allowed us the opportunity to get to know one another and make a special connection that would last our lifetimes.

Yesterday, Today, and Forever

by Sharon Rhyce

Hearing the word cancer is a gut punch.

How on earth has it been fifty-three years since I, Bert Martinez, a 73-year-old, married this woman? My sweet and precious best friend, Brenda reminds me, "Time goes by so fast, Bert. I've been blessed, no – we've been blessed with a great life together. We've had good health until recently, until I got the "C-word" from Dr. Sols."

"So true, but when we take good care of ourselves, eat right, watch our weight, exercise, and do all the doctor visits – your diagnosis came out of the blue," I respond as we watch the waves in their rhythmic pattern on Crescent Beach. Despite the previous months of turmoil and fear, we both recognize that we have had good fortune to have Brenda receive excellent care at Moffitt Cancer Center.

Brenda then reminds me, "Fate had a hand in this, Bert. If not for that earthquake in January of 2020, I would not have visited my doctor until June, upon our return from Puerto Rico," Brenda sighs. I know she is right. That earthquake ruined our annual plans for sure, or so we thought. I was terribly disappointed when canceling these travel plans that we looked forward to every single year for the past twenty years or so. We visited the homeland of my mother each year with great anticipation. Brenda and I found solace visiting Puerto Rico for three months after the hustle of the holidays were over. "I can't believe our plans are ruined due to the earthquake," I pouted.

Brenda, ever the optimist, shrugged, "There's always next year." Little did we know then that this burst bubble would be such an incredible blessing. "That earthquake saved me, I bumped up my doctor appointment by five full months all because we did not go to Puerto Rico," Brenda reminds me. She is right. By going to see her doctor in January instead of June, Brenda's cancer was caught early. We'd been married over fifty years now and this news rocked our world.

I would pray and beg both God and Science to help us. I say help us because she is my everything. She is my life, my rock, my world. So many emotions came at the forefront of the year. I am saddened, no one likes to hear the word cancer.

I am so grateful; this woman has changed my life making me whole and complete. I am in awe. Every story has a beginning and I look back to the start of our story. I find it surreal how all the stars aligned that day. Fifty-plus years and my mind drifts back to 1966 and the day we met. A simpler time when Ed Sullivan ruled our Sunday evenings, guys used Brylcreem, Elvis was king, Johnson was president, the Viet-Nam war was ratcheting, girls wore long hair and short skirts, and my life was about to change forever.

During my high school years, I was an athlete, fitting in nicely after transplanting from New York my freshman year. I enjoyed playing both baseball and football for the Chiefs. I was young and perhaps a bit full of myself as I look back. At the time, I knew athletes had some understood privileges. Academics were of a secondary nature, taking a backseat to my all-important world of athletics. I did fine in all my classes, but I put most of my effort into my first loves - baseball and football, in that order.

Now that I was a senior, I was at the pinnacle of my career as a jock, a big man on campus. I thought nothing of leaving class a little earlier than the crowd, and I relished being able to beat the bell. This allowed me the luxury to meander down the near empty hallways. I could stop at my locker more often and carry a lot less. Being the good student that I was, most teachers would not bat an eye. I was now used to this privilege given to very few. Frankly, plain and simple, I earned it.

The picture in my mind is crystal clear to this day. I had decided to leave my history class a few minutes early since my teacher gave us an assignment to work on. Mr. Caves saw me close my book and I gave him a thumbs up. He nodded and I proceeded out the door.

I walked down the corridor and after stopping at my locker, I turned right to head upstairs to my next class. At the very top of the stairs stood a young lady. I managed a look that soaked it all in – long blonde hair, a skirt that fell above her knees, the palest, fairest face with doe eyes that would make Bambi jealous and a ruffled top that softly exuded femininity and gentleness.

She had not one armful of books, but two. Within mere seconds of wondering why she was so loaded down; my answer was provided. A young man appeared behind her, and my zeal quickly waned. Clearly this site I was beholding was out of my league. I recognized him; he was a football player on the junior varsity team. My thoughts were that she was not only kind and sweet for walking this junior varsity player, she had to be very responsible; for this young man was on crutches. I surmised the teachers trusted her to the task.

That day changed me. While the feeling was like no other, words cannot describe the feelings that stirred within me. Nothing else mattered. Up to now, my life had been school with sports being the main draw, academics secondary, and a goal of working to soup up my car and drive to my part time job that provided any extras I wanted. The sight of this young lady just made everything else disappear. I don't know how to fully describe the change within me in that moment. I was awestruck. She was the answer and up until then I didn't have a question!

I managed to continue up the stairs quickly for fear that this beautiful tall blonde goddess would be able to read my mind. My feet felt like they were filled with lead. *Move it, Bert. You've got this,* I thought to myself. I was not worthy of even a glance at her as I neared the top of the stairs. I continued to my math class with the most awesome vision implanted in my brain. I want to say it was her hair, no – her gentle manner as she carried all those books with such finesse, but I think the doe eyes did me in. Perhaps it was all three...

I arrived early to class and took my seat as soon as the current class of students emptied into the corridor. My feet had successfully taken me on this road well-traveled, my brain, however, was not connected to my body, or so it seemed. I could not think about anything but what had occurred moments ago in the stairwell. Was I dreaming? No, I knew what I saw. Every time I thought of this girl, I added more descriptors; pretty, no, drop dead gorgeous, long hair, no, shiny blonde hair...

I envisioned her over and over in my mind like a play by play that NFL referees watch. My view too was on repeat. My best friend Fred was in my math class, and I later learned he tried to get my attention to no avail. As soon as class was over, Fred was about to talk to me and I interrupted him.

"Fred, there's this girl...I've never seen her before, and she is so beautiful."

Fred gave me a huge grin and a light slap on the back as he chortled, "What's gotten into you, brother? This is a side of you I've never seen. Looks like cupid shot that arrow!"

Fred and I continued our way to our next class, downstairs. Fred and I were just about to part ways at the same location as we did every school day.

I heard the chatter of gym class and glanced to my right. There she was! I called Fred back over and words stumbled. Lips closed in ventriloquist fashion, I declared, "That's her! That's her!"

She wore a marshmallow white, one-piece jump suit with pouf-like shorts secured by elastic at the bottom and empty white cloth belt loops in the middle. She had white socks on, and her sneakers were white canvas, the kind with a white cloth tongue that sat under the tied laces. Remembering her gracefulness at the top of the stairs earlier and this vision in white before me reminded me of an angel. There she was an angel in my midst! I caught a glimpse of her, and she tried to hide behind some other students. *Great, she is avoiding me.*

Fred piped in, "I know her."

Sweet Jesus, Fred knows this cutie pie!

He continued, "That's my new girlfriend's kid sister."

I begged Fred, "Please, please I need you to arrange for me to meet her. You've got connections! That gorgeous girl is your Susie's kid sister! Help me please."

"Of course, that's what friends are for," Fred immediately snickers, "How can I not help my buddy when Cupid's arrow has been shot?"

Fred set a plan in motion; "Leave it to me, Bert. I'll get my new girlfriend, Susie, to get her kid sister to meet us."

I immediately interrupt Fred. "Are you for real? Are you sure you can pull this off? What do I need to do? I'll do anything..."

"Geez Louise, let me clue you in on my plan," Fred continues, "I'll get Susie to meet us at the intersection of the cafeteria and the art wing. We can put this plan in place today."

"T-t-t-today?" I stammered.

I recall Fred mentioning some smart aleck remark, "Nah, I thought we should wait until Christmas," as he shakes his head and puts forth his mischievous grin and we part ways.

The plan is all set. I plan to meet them at the designated intersection right before noon. Fred is like a brother to me ever since I moved from the Big Apple to the Magic City. His dad is my baseball coach and a true father figure. Fred's family has been a real plus since day one, but this, this was HUGE! Icing on the cake for sure.

Meanwhile, my lead feet attempted to move to my next class. I struggled to remove myself from this most pleasant view of a goddess in white. She rocked in that gym suit! One more class to go and perhaps Fred could work his magic. Time never moved so darn slow.

I thought it would never end, but at last, my class was over. I took my BMOC (big man on campus) attitude along with my new excitement out of the classroom. With a spring in my step, leaving early of course, I anxiously awaited the opportunity to meet this girl close up.

I raced to the art wing, arriving at the last perpendicular walkway where we agreed to meet. All three walked towards me, but I only had eyes for the young lady.

Should I wave? *Down boy*, I thought to myself.

Should I smile? *Too friendly and too eager,* I decided.

My heart pounded, racing fiercely. There, within a few feet, stood the trio. I was so excited and filled with more anticipation than had I been sitting behind home plate watching the Yankees play a baseball game.

Fred casually introduced me to Susie, his new girlfriend. His words sputtered out in a forced nonchalant manner, "Susie, this here is my buddy, Bert." I gave a nonchalant wave as I whispered a very soft, "Hey there." I soaked in the sight before me as I saw Brenda with her older sister Susie. My eyes were quicker than my speech. I found it difficult to breathe, my brain could not process, and my heart was a-flutter. Yet my eyes were working simply fine, thank you very much.

She wore cordovan brown penny loafers with the penny in the appropriate slits at the top of her shoes. Her deep maroon skirt rested slightly above her knees providing a view of her long legs. The soft pink blouse matched her skirt perfectly and was the epitome of her femininity. Her blonde hair sparkled and shone with brilliance and cascaded down her back, with the ends flipped up. Her doe eyes were amber colored and had me mesmerized.

My mouth was slower than a three-legged turtle. Fred had already introduced me to Brenda, and I was not able to multi-task. I looked but could not speak I wanted to shake her hand, but mine remained frozen at my side.

Fred gave me quizzical looks, and I knew I was messing this up. Susie smiled, Brenda smiled, and Fred likely thought I was a real dork. This party of four was about to disband, Fred placing his arm behind Susie's back as they started to leave. Brenda too turned in the opposite direction.

Faster than Elvis could say, "Thankyouverymuch," I managed to spill out, "Can I walk you to class?"

Luckily, those gorgeous doe eyes looked at me and said, "Sure."

I walked Brenda to her Civics class, slowly. Still soaking it all in. My eyes continued to work faster than my speech. "I had Civics last year," I stuttered.

"Really? That's nice." Brenda responded in the softest and sweetest voice.

"I had Mr. Allen for Civics," I add.

"I think he's the only one that teaches it," Brenda states as I want to crawl into a hole.

As we approach Brenda's class, I look at her for a quick second and say, "Here's your class." *What on earth was I thinking?*

Brenda manages a quick, "Bye, thanks."

As Brenda walks into class, I realize the angel of my dreams is gone- forever. I have been the klutz of all klutzes. I will be lucky to see her from a far at best, I am sure of it.

It was crazy how *my* actions became a blur after all these years. Brenda's words however are etched in stone, and I remember everything about her as if it were yesterday. I know I messed up my chances, I'm sure I've let Fred down and I know any hope with Brenda is now history. Then I went to the other side of the school to get my books for my next class. I was running late, but I did not care. Nothing mattered except Brenda.

At times, Cupid's arrow hits hard, and for me, it most certainly did. I felt as though neither time, nor space prior to the moment on the stairwell even mattered. I had a rebirth of sorts, and my life was simply fine! I had to bump into Brenda again, and I was hellbent on not making it my last encounter. I could not strike out. And so far, I was not doing well. This was not a simple game of baseball we were talking about!

I had to get it together and breathe and calm down.

The next day, I felt much better. Hope was alive! I purposely encountered Brenda carrying the junior varsity football player's books and managed to intentionally repeat the previous day. This time my feet felt a bit lighter, and I managed a "Hi there," and even made small talk with the guy on crutches. I had an opportunity to fix my mess from the day before.

Upon seeing her at gym later, I gave a friendly wave and quite a shout out, "Hey Brenda!" I then caught up with Fred. I told Fred, "I can't mess this up. Walking her to class yesterday I was awful. I got tongue tied and I am still embarrassed. "

Fred reminded me, "You'll be fine. Brenda is really sweet, and her sister Susie told me Brenda likes you."

"Look, don't make stuff up to make me feel better, Fred," I insisted.

"I am one hundred percent serious," Fred looks me square in the eye. I know he is telling me the truth.

Ecstatic doesn't begin to describe it; I have been given a second chance with the first girl ever to mean the world to me!

Brenda did not hide this time, she waved back. Before I speak up, Brenda pipes in,

"How are you, Bert?" asks Brenda.

"I'm great, how are you doing?" I question, knowing this requires a response, affording me the opportunity to hear her voice again.

Brenda then informs me, "I'm doing fine. Should we meet Susie at the same spot as yesterday?"

Fred states, "I'll walk Susie over so we can all be together." Fred is truly my savior!

The four of us met at the same intersection as the day before, only this time I was encouraged by Brenda's "interest" in me.

I manage a quick and perky, "Hi Susie" when she arrives. I add a grin for good measure.

We talk and I don't mess up this time around!

I ask Brenda what she does after school and she adds, "I work after school from four to nine at J. Byrons. Then I have homework and babysit on weekends whenever I can."

I then explain, "I have practice after school just about every day. I get home late and then do my homework. On weekends I work to pay for my Chevelle SS. I'm wanting to buy the tiger that goes on top of the back seat console."

Brenda adds, "I've seen those tigers, they are cool, the way the eyes light up when you're going to turn."

"That's right," I add, "The eyes work in tandem with the turn signals. Left eye blinks when I turn left, right eye blinks when I turn right and both eyes will light up when I put on my brakes or slow down."

Brenda questions me, "Do you install it yourself?"

"It's an easy install," I reply.

"Wow, that's very cool" Brenda smiles.

Bonus points for me, things are starting to look up. My confidence is building. I go for the jugular. "I know you're pretty busy but are you ever free on the weekends?"

Brenda adds, "Only when I don't have a babysitting job, which doesn't happen often."

In chatting, I realized we both worked outside of school, and my sports did not allow us much time to be together except for at school.

"Well, our time certainly is limited. Can I walk you to your Civics class?" I ask.

My heart raced as she replied with a smile, "Of course you can!"

This feeling is way better than getting an autographed baseball from Mickey Mantle! For the remainder of the school year, we followed this ritualistic schedule. We squeezed lunch in as well. I'd save her a seat and we'd eat our bag lunches side by side. The more I got to know Brenda, the more I knew she was the one that completed me. We spent as much time as we could together, mostly in the hallway or lunchroom.

For the remainder of my senior year, we remained inseparable. We became best friends. I had my part time job which afforded me the luxury of paying for my 1966 Chevelle, a fine muscle car with a maroon exterior and a white interior. Even now, this car brings back wonderful memories. Between our jobs and my sports, there was minimal time. I was not able to afford to take Brenda on costly dates. Our parents needed us to work if we wanted anything "extra" as our family lived paycheck to paycheck, barely scraping by. We often spent our time at the local burger joints back in the day—Royal Castle, Burger King, Lums, or any place that was cheap. Neither food nor venue mattered, only Brenda did. We talked and laughed for hours not realizing how quickly time flew by.

A few months later, I graduated and went on to attend a local community college. Soon enough I found that college was not my thing. I went to work for the construction company building I-95 through downtown Miami. I worked full time on the survey crew and enjoyed it very much. Brenda and I continued to see each other during her junior and senior year. She was everything I could dream of and more. I knew she was "the one." We both knew we were meant to be!

Our engagement was not a formal event. Her prom, junior prom, was the time we got engaged. There wasn't any fanfare like engagements of today. The ring I gave Brenda had a miniscule diamond that one almost needed a microscope to see. It was all I could afford and no one else knew the symbolism of the ring. Being that the diamond was so small, her parents and mine, along with our friends thought nothing of it – it was merely a friendship ring. Brenda and I knew better though. Fred and Susie knew we vowed to marry one day, and they shared in our joy and secret. As was common at the time, once graduation for Brenda came, we would tie the knot. I remember sitting in my car after prom as music played and we rolled out our life plans before us. I reached into my tux pocket and placed the tiny ring on her finger after I popped the question. Without hesitation, Brenda said, "Yes." We had less hoopla for our engagement than kids get when they graduate from elementary school nowadays. We didn't need the fancy and the fluff, we had each other. Perhaps this was a prelude of our life to come. We STILL don't need fancy, we have each other.

Just as when we were "kids" and knew what we really needed was each other, hope and love...cancer reminds us our needs haven't changed at all. We've got each other, we have hope, and we most certainly have love.

Living the Story

All the
Ordinary Moments

by Miranda Scotti

He's wearing the green shirt.

The thought swirls into my mind as I open the front door and take in the sight of Joey, pacing along the stoop in his black-rimmed glasses. His hands are tucked deep into the pockets of his dark skinny jeans, and the summer sun reflects the scattered red specks of his short brown hair. To anyone else, it might seem like he's wearing an ordinary t-shirt, but I know it means more than that to him. It's a forest green, 60/40 cotton polyester blend, his favorite color and preferred textile combination. It's also the same shirt he wore on our first date, which is the fact that I'm currently hyper focused on as I stand here in a purple dress, the same color I wore that night. The thought settles down somewhere deep in my chest as he turns toward me. When our eyes meet, I try to read him, to decipher whether he chose his outfit purposefully.

"Happy birthday," he says, a shy smile on his lips. He takes two steps toward me and I wrap my arms around his shoulders and inhale. He smells like mountain spring deodorant, fresh laundry detergent, and french fries.

"Thanks," I grin up at him. "Did you stop at Wendy's on the way to pick me up for my birthday lunch?"

Pale pink splotches bloom across his cheekbones. "How did you know?"

I brush a few crumbs off his shirt. "For one thing, you stop at Wendy's on your way everywhere. Also, you smell like french fries."

He shrugs and tilts his head to the side, his right dimple winking down at me. "What can I say?"

I scrunch my nose and grin, trying to read him again. His smile is timid, there's a faint amount of stubble spread across his cheeks and upper lip, and it looks like he got his hair trimmed, but what I really can't stop thinking about is the fact that he's wearing that shirt. It's already taken up spot number three on my subliminal list of reasons I think *maybe* I'll end up engaged by the end of the day:

1. He asked me to take the day off work because he planned a surprise.
2. He's filled with adorable nervous energy.
3. He's wearing the first date shirt.

I try to shake the thoughts out of my head. It all suddenly seems absurd.

Joey and I have been together for almost ten months now, but we were friends for years before we started dating. He worked downtown, with my two best friends and we had only spent time together in group settings before last October. When we both found ourselves single, after untangling from long term relationships, we tried to stay just friends. But late-night Instant Message chats about everything and nothing quickly turned into a plan to grab pizza, just the two of us. My friends laughed at me for obsessing over whether it was a date or not as I got ready, but just like today, as soon as I opened the front door and saw him standing there in that green shirt, I knew it was a date just by the way he smiled at me, like he felt every bit as hopeful as I did.

But that was only ten months ago, and even though I've experienced some of the best moments of my life during that time, and, sure, we've talked about how we want to get married someday, it's probably presumptuous to think that he'd propose so soon. We spend almost every night either at my house or his apartment, but we don't even live together yet. Plus, Joey almost exclusively wears t-shirts, so my theory is pretty weak. It's a humid day and I know how he feels about the cotton-polyester blend. He's probably just going for comfort. Just because I fixated over what to wear today, I shouldn't assume that he's the kind of person who chooses an outfit so carefully. He probably won't even notice that I happen to be in a purple dress. I wouldn't even want him to, because then he might know that I suspect this is more than a birthday date.

I'm probably overthinking this. I tend to overthink everything.

"You look beautiful," he says, interrupting my spiraling thoughts. "New dress?"

Okay, so he *is* the kind of guy who pays attention to clothing choices. It's just a simple cotton A-line dress with cap sleeves. A summer dress. I didn't necessarily expect him to notice it was new, but I really shouldn't be surprised. Joey is an observer, one of the many things I love about him. His thoughtful and honest nature has drawn me to him from the beginning. He's always pointing out little details about things around us that I might miss otherwise, like which planets are visible in the sky on any given night, or how the lizard that lives on my front porch has a red head. He can take one look at me and tell if I'm having a pain flare, even if I'm smiling and trying to hide it. He knows me almost as well as I know myself, a realization that makes me pause. Does this mean he probably knows about this list I've been keeping in my head all week? There's no way he can tell that I'm suspicious. *Right?*

I bite my lip, one of my many nervous habits. "Yup, new dress."

He catches my gaze. "It's purple, like you wore on our first date."

Nodding my head rapidly, I remind my eyes to remain in their sockets and not give me away. I carefully hide my hands behind my back, so he won't notice that I also got a just-in-case manicure.

"And I'm wearing my favorite green shirt," he says.

Now my heart is pinballing around in my chest and I can't tell whether he thinks it's a coincidence or he's giving me some kind of clue. He's probably worn that shirt once a week since we started dating. My brain decides to remind me he's just pointing out that I got a new dress because it's my birthday. Not just any birthday, either. I'm twenty-four on the 24th. My Golden Birthday. That's why he's making this a big deal. That's all. Nothing else.

"Can't beat the 60/40 cotton-poly blend," I say, not sure whether I sound nonchalant or like I'm about to faint.

His smile widens and I already know exactly what he's going to say. He knows I know, because he says it every time, but he says it anyway, just to make me smile. "The perfect combination of comfort and breathability to combat the Florida humidity."

I laugh, despite the nerves tingling throughout my body. I should just be enjoying this day, not worrying about how it might turn out. In the past ten months, Joey and I have been through so much together. My world has changed dramatically, not just because I found my soulmate, but because wrapped up in the joy of falling in love, there's been so much pain. Chronic, physical pain, with no end. My life has been a revolving door of specialist appointments recently, trying to figure out why I suddenly started experiencing constant nerve pain about eight months ago. He's been by my side every step of the way. He researched until he found the specialist who finally diagnosed me. He stuck with me after I was told that Interstitial Cystitis and Fibromyalgia, while not life-threatening, are incurable chronic conditions. There's a chance I'll never feel like my old self again, so we go on mini adventures on the good days, and he listens to me cry on the bad ones. We help each other find silver linings when life gets us down.

I don't know what it would be like to go through this without him, but what I do know is that no matter what, I want us, side-by-side, forever. I'm a daydreamer by nature, but I've never been one to fanaticize about a grand proposal or a fancy wedding. I just want a simple life with Joey, filled with laughter and love, and I want to start planning that life as soon as possible.

Joey clears his throat and interrupts my spinning thoughts again. "Ready to go?"

My eyes flutter up to his, but he's looking down at his sneakers now. If I had to guess, his brain is running its own marathon. I can't help but hope that they have the same destination.

"Mmmhmm." I shake my head way more times than necessary. "Let's go."

Filled with a mixture of elation and nerves, I climb into his car. I glance in the backseat and see the vintage picnic basket I got him for his birthday. I packed a lunch and took him to our favorite tree that day. I wasn't feeling well, but we made the best of it, and I'm extra thankful that today is a low pain day for me. He asked me a few weeks ago if I could take today off work because he had a surprise planned. I'm the kind of girl who normally doesn't like surprises, too much anxiety and all that, but it's different with him. He first showed me I could trust him back when we were just friends, and countless times since we first kissed under the same tree that I hope we're heading toward now.

If he's planning a surprise, it's going to be a good one.

I mentally add this new information to my list:

4. Picnic basket in the back seat means we're (maybe? probably?) having a picnic under our tree.

I'm ridiculous.

Joey catches me looking at the basket and lets out a half-laugh. "You can probably guess where we're going."

"To our tree?"

He backs out of my driveway with a pensive grin. "Where else?"

The drive from my downtown Orlando bungalow to the park is technically only one mile, but it manages to feel like a lifetime. Jens Lekman's mellow Swedish voice is singing sweetly to us through the car speakers and our hands are intertwined and resting on the center console. He drives carefully over a speed bump, but it still causes me to wince and squeeze his hand. He glances at me. "You okay?"

I shut my eyes and nod, as sharp pains zings through me, then dissipates. I shift to a more comfortable position in the seat as we drive past the former location of Will's Pub, the dive bar where we first met three years earlier. My best friend invited me to meet up with her and some friends from work after my box office shift at the local indie movie theater. She introduced us under the hazy bar lights, as their coworker's band finished their set. It would be another year before Joey and I became good friends, and a year beyond that before we'd spend our evenings chatting online about music and life into the early hours of the morning. By that time, the pub had closed and moved to a new location.

"I still can't believe they tore down Will's and turned it into a parking lot," he says.

I contort my whole face in frustration. "A parking lot for a doctor who misdiagnosed me, no less."

"Hey," he glances over at me, his face soft. "We're proof that you can't pave over what matters, right?"

I'm thankful he catches me before I slip into frustration. We're good at that; reminding each other to be optimistic when one of loses our grip on the hope that bound us together in the first place. I take a steady breath and smile at him. "That's true. Long live Will's."

"Cheers," he says, raising an invisible pint glass, then taking my hand gently in his again.

He's right. Between the time we met there and the time we started dating, the bar closed, a chapter ending. But a few years later they moved to a new location, just down the road. It reminds me that every ending leaves space for a whole new beginning. No matter what, that spot would always be our first beginning, paving the way for days like today.

Or at least I hope so.

When we reach the parking lot facing our tree, he pulls into the same spot we parked the night of our first date. I wonder if it's deliberate, but I remind myself it's a small parking lot and there really aren't that many options.

We walk slowly toward the tree in a silence that's not unpleasant, but the tension between us has grown palpable. Dry leaves crunch under my thin white sandals as I duck under lush branches, following Joey through the familiar path beneath the tree. I dodge some overgrown roots, reminding myself it's not an ideal time to trip and fall, although I suspect he finds my clumsiness at least a little endearing.

Holding on tight to the old picnic basket, Joey turns and smiles shyly, his prominent dimple gleaming at me. "Almost there."

We arrive at a shaded spot suitable for a picnic, and the wind whistles through the branches, as if playing a sappy love song just for us. I think back to the first time we came here together. After eating at a local pizzeria that drizzly fall evening, I suggested we drive to the park so I could show him something amazing. I knew him well enough to know he'd be impressed by the expansive tree, penned as "The Mayor" by locals. It's the kind of tree that takes your breath away when you realize it's so massive that most of its limbs have grown back into the ground. Some don't even stop there, weaving their way over and under, holding each other up. It's hard to tell where the roots begin and end, but it's obvious that their bond is enduring. Together, they're unyielding.

Joey looks up at me, his dark brown eyes focused on mine. "Is this good?" he asks.

I smile and nod my head. "It's just right."

Of course it is. He always takes care to make sure every little detail of everything we do is just right for us. Whether it's making sure I'm comfortable in a car or confirming we're going to a restaurant that has something I can eat on my new medical diet. On the days I'm too weak to worry about myself, he's always there to lighten the load for me and bring bright spots to the gloomy times we face. More than anything, he makes the most of all the ordinary moments right along with me.

I balance on one of the many overgrown roots of the giant tree while Joey concentrates on placing a dark green picnic blanket next to a pile of fallen acorns. I settle down next to him and stare up at the impossibly clear cerulean sky peeking through the canopy of the tree. There are no dark clouds today. It's a typical July afternoon in Orlando, which is to say hot. But it's the kind of day that has felt full of hope from the moment I woke up and the sunlight seeped into my eyes through the half-broken blinds covering my window.

Joey's sneakers tap against the picnic blanket as I settle in and shift into a comfortable position. I wonder what song is going through his head. Sometimes he gets as lost in the music playing in his mind as I get in my daydreams. But today, while I'm staring up at the tree, Joey is focused on me and only me.

"You feeling okay?" he asks.

I force a smile in his direction, even though we both know it's been a long time since I've felt *okay*. We'd only been dating two months when the pain started taking over my life. Even though we were already serious, I struggled to understand why Joey stayed by my side at first, when I was so miserable and obviously wasn't getting better. It took time for me to accept that he saw me as more than my pain, and I began to realize that if the situation was reversed, I would feel the same way. The explanation is simple, as far as I can see.

He loves me as much as I love him.

I know it with every squeeze of his hand when I'm hurting, every moment he spends researching ways to reduce my pain, every smile he gives me during the best days and the hardest ones, too. In the deepest part of my heart, I know we were part of a secret society of people who truly understand the meaning of soulmates. Together, our roots have grown as strong as the tree.

Our tree.

It's lost limbs to outside forces like hurricanes and internal forces like old age. Still, it stands rooted in the park, a tree that passersby can't help but stop to admire. A tree that has been through so much, but lives on, thriving when it can and letting its limbs rest when necessary.

"I'm good," I smile back at him.

Pain aside, it's a lovely afternoon. Summer in Florida means it's too hot to be outside in the middle of the day unless you've found a shady spot to hide from the sweltering sun. The park is mostly empty besides a few joggers along the sidewalk every now and then, getting in their runs before the daily afternoon rain begins. Love birds chirp at us from their nests high in the sturdy branches of the tree as we eat the Publix subs he's packed for us for lunch. Sunlight filters through the branches and paints bold yellow patches in the grass and dirt surrounding us. Golden birthday, indeed.

A placard nearby boasts the tree has been here since 1688, the same year Sir Isaac Newton published his law of universal gravitation. The law explains exactly how strong the gravitational force between two masses must be to attract each other, and next to that very sign is the spot we first kissed.

How appropriate.

Swallowing a bite of my sub, I tap my foot against his. "I'm glad it's not raining like the first time we came here. Remember how frizzy my hair got? I thought it was going to take over the whole park."

He laughs, nearly choking on a bite of his sandwich. "It looked like you stuck your finger in a light socket."

"I think it managed to defy Newton's law of gravity by epic proportions," I elbow him playfully, "but it didn't scare you off."

Pink passes from his cheeks all the way to his ears. I love that after all we've been through, I can still make him blush. I lean into his shoulder and his familiar Joey scent fills me up. He runs his fingers through my hair, which I spent an hour straightening this morning to avoid another light socket scenario.

"Not at all. I loved it," he says, kissing the side of my head.

My cheeks flush in kind and I gaze at my freshly painted nails again. I once told him if he ever proposed, I didn't want a diamond. A few days later he asked if I'd feel differently if he could find one that was ethically sourced. That's Joey. He loves solutions. Since then, I can't help but imagine a ring there sometimes. Something tangible to carry with me wherever I go, a reminder of everything we've been through and whatever we might face in the future. I know choosing to spend our lives together means we'll face tons of unknowns. There's no doubt we can do it though. I believe we can get through anything together. Illness, loss, unexpected tragedies. I bet we could even survive a global pandemic if we had to.

I steal a glimpse back at Joey, careful not to make it obvious I was checking out my ring finger. His feet are still dancing around and I can tell from his barely eaten sub and the way he's slouching that he's getting antsy. We're having a perfectly good time, but he's more quiet than usual. We're close enough that I can feel the nervous energy rising and falling from in his chest.

"You okay?" I ask quietly, turning to face him as I cross my legs.

He gulps and his eyes dart around the park. "Uh, yeah. Are you up for a walk?"

My heart starts dancing. Not a slow dance either, more like a polka. "Like on our first date?"

His Adam's apple bobs up and down as he shakes his head and stands. I secretly examine all his pockets, but there is definitely not a ring box hiding anywhere in his skinny jeans. I throw this observation on my mental list of reasons I'm probably *not* getting engaged today, and I reach for his hand so he can help me up. I have to move carefully to avoid pain flares. Sitting down, standing up, walking, driving around. It all causes me nerve pain throughout my entire body like needles and pins constantly poking my arms and legs. The slower and more thoughtfully I move, the less likely I am to end up needing to go home and take a nap.

Wiping away some crumbs and dirt, I straighten out my dress. Joey points his head toward a path that leads to the bridge we walked over on that warm October night. The night of our first date, our first kiss.

"This way," he says.

As we make our way out from under the canopy of our tree, the blaring sunlight beats down against our backs. I wonder if that's why Joey's palms are sweating... or could it be something more? I still can't decide, and I want my brain to let me live in the moment, knowing it doesn't really matter either way. We stroll through a winding path, past a folk-art museum, and beyond a gazebo that overlooks a crystal-clear lake. He's recreating the first walk we took here. Soon we're standing on the bridge, staring out to where the sidewalk disappears.

"This is where we first held hands, remember?" he asks.

I squeeze his hand. "I'd been waiting all night for that."

I'd been waiting much longer than just a few hours actually. The weeks before we finally admitted our feelings to each other and decided to go out were slow and intense— kind of like this birthday walk we're taking. The walk I so desperately want to be *more* than just a birthday walk. We've talked about the future plenty, how there's no version of it either of us can imagine without the other as our partner in life. Our hopes and dreams and plans all align just right. Even with my condition, a life together is what we both want more than anything.

"Let's keep walking," he says, after we watch a canoe glide past on the lake. He gestures toward a sidewalk that leads back around the tree. More specifically, to the spot where we first kissed. This is just a super romantic and sweet date, I remind myself again. His hand is probably shaking a little because he wants the day to be perfect.

It's quiet as we walk the path under the bright sun. When we cross beneath a giant branch that's grown high enough over the sidewalk to create a walkway, we're suddenly back under the shade of the tree and almost to our spot.

"Remember our first kiss?" he asks quietly, ducking under a stray branch.

My voice is as shaky as his hand and I whisper back, "How could I forget?"

I remember every second of that night.

Every moment we shared leading up to it.

And every single one since.

Because falling in love is a process. One that starts before you even realize it's happening. And it goes at its own pace. You can't rush it because if it's not the right time, or if it's not the right person, then it's never going to be right. But once it is, there's no slowing it down, and before you know it, you're standing under the most extraordinary tree on a humid fall night in October with your perfect match, the one who understands you best, the one who will love all the broken pieces of you enough it won't even matter if they never fit back together quite the same again. That's what I learned that night.

And maybe the beginning was nearly two years earlier, a quarter mile away, at the ghost of the pub where we first met. Or the offer of a ride home when I was feeling lost and alone. Sharing all the perfect songs at just the right moments. The steady beat of keys tapping out the gotchas and yeps and yeahs and hms from the dark of night into the blurred light of the morning. A knock at the door because he'd arrived for our first date. Sitting under a gazebo with my head on his shoulder. Walking around the park discovering that our hands fit together just right. It was all the ordinary moments we'd shared that led us to the tree. It was the kiss that told me it was going to be forever.

Lost in the memories of how it all began, I almost don't realize we've arrived at our spot. It barely registers that he's kneeling down next to the very same crack in the sidewalk where we first leaned into each other and kissed. He looks up at me, his thin frame balancing on one knee, dark brown eyes piercing through me, a sparkling ring in his hand, that's apparently been hiding in the coin pocket of his jeans all along. It's stunning, but nowhere near as beautiful as this person who I've known is my soulmate since the first time we stood here. His words whirl around me and out into the ether.

"I've loved you every day since our first date, and I know I am going to love you forever. Will you marry me?"

The song my heart plays now reaches my toes, and they dance around, pulling him up as fast as I can.

"Of course, I'll marry you!"

I'm not worried about pain or being careful right now, because all I can do is grin and giggle and thank the moon and all the constellations and the universe's gravitational pull for bringing us together. A honk from a car driving by interrupts our moment. The passenger whistles and whoops and we chuckle and wave.

I stop to admire my new ring as he explains it's certified conflict-free, and once again his thoughtfulness makes me dizzy with joy. It's a round diamond on a white gold band with six prongs holding it in tight.

"Like a tiger's claw," he laughs, imitating the guy at the jewelry store we visited a few months earlier.

Shaking my head and letting out a stream of chuckles, I reach up and pull his cheeks towards my lips.

"Kiss me again," I whisper.

One of his hands cradles the back of my head and with the other, he pulls out a digital camera from my purse and snaps a flawless engagement photo.

Most things in life are far from perfect. My health, our jobs, us as human beings with all our flaws. But I believe no matter what we face—the best days, the hard times, the perfectly mundane moments—we might not realize we'll miss until they're gone. Through all of it, we're perfect for each other.

We break apart long enough for Joey to look up through the branches and then back down at me again. He raises his right eyebrow and his dimple goes with it. "We're getting married under this tree."

I smile up at him, the leaves and roots and branches reflecting back at me through his glasses. "You think we can fit both sides of our giant Italian families under here?"

He tucks a stray strand of hair behind my ear and shrugs. "We'll find a way."

And I know it's true, because we always do.

The Love Story of Margrethe

by Madonna Dries Christensen

Visalia, California, 17 January, 1917

Dear Sister:

First of all, best wishes

Margrethe Christensen stopped. The nib on her pen had dripped blue ink on the page. She wiped the pen, and reached for a clean sheet of stationary. This letter would be difficult; a story she must explain. She needed to get her ducks in a row as to how it all came about. To clear her mind, she paced the floor, reflecting on her seemingly endless trip across the uncertain sea, then across the great expanse of the United States, to California. She had mailed a note to her parents in Denmark, saying she had arrived safely but things had not gone as planned with Hans. There was more to tell. Much more.

Margrethe intended this letter for her twin, Dagmar, but now decided it would go to her older sister, Johanne, who would read it to her parents and siblings. Johanne liked being in charge; the first to know details. She was single, a romantic, flirtatious; she would relish the letter's content. Dagmar was shy and had as yet shown little interest in having a beau. The oldest sister, Ane Margrethe, named for their mother, was already five years married, but it had never seemed to Margrethe to have been a love match. They had no children yet and seemed old before their time. Yes, it was Johanne to whom she would write. Before continuing, her memories rolled back to childhood, when the idea of emigrating first occurred.

Aarre, Denmark, 1906

She'd been eleven-years-old. She and Dagmar and Johanne and their older brother, Kristian, sat together at a Going To America party for a family friend, Peder Marinus Madsen. Marinus, as he preferred to be called, had apprenticed to his uncle, the village cobbler. Here at the barn dance, there was food, drink, lively music and dancing to the accompaniment of a mandolin, two fiddles, an accordion, and a concertina. Each man seemed to be playing his own tune. *Mor* danced with their oldest sibling, Ole Peder. Their father, Zacharias, had gone outside with friends to smoke; only a fool would smoke in a barn. Especially barns attached to the house, as they were here.

Johanne, eyeing Marinus, said, "He's handsome and has a nice manner." At twelve, she was mature for her age, and already boys were taking a second look at her. "It's strange he hasn't married. He's twice my age and then some."

"He's twenty-seven," Kristian said.

Joanne thumped his head. "As I said. Twice my age and then some."

"That's not so old. *Far* was thirty-three when he married *Mor*. And if Marinus marries, his children will always have shoes." Kristian laughed at his joke.

"He needs a wife to put meat on his bones. At least he's not getting soused like some of the men."

Kristian grinned. "Once, I sneaked a couple of sips of aquavit and had to lie down the rest of the day. My head was swimming. I told *Mor* I had a belly ache, and I did."

Margrethe leaned her head against Dagmar, their pale blonde curls blending into a swirl like cake frosting. "I want to go to America," she said with a sigh. "I want to see the bigger world."

"I'm going," Kristian said. "That's for sure."

Dagmar told him, "*Far* says Ole Peder will tend the farm and you will stay here and study to become a pastor."

Kristian scoffed. "I will study law, not religion." At fifteen, he seemed to know his future.

Three years later, he refused a minister's life, and *Far* withheld funds to study law. Two stubborn men who would not bend. Kristian left home at seventeen, spending time in England, and then to America. In his letters to the family, he wrote of his adventures. Johanne said, "He's always been a rascal, our family *nisse*."

"Fairy tales," *Far* muttered. "He's on his own and must behave like an adult."

Johanne read from his letter, "I arrived in Boston early in the day. The immigrants were sent to a barracks with floor to ceiling windows, like a tobacco barn. We had to remain there until our name was called, which might take a day or two. I convinced a friend that it was silly to wait so we stepped out a window and toured Boston. We were lucky to return just before our names were called and we were processed out the door, legally."

Far frowned. "Perhaps he should study law. He's already into mischief and he was vague about some problem in England."

The letter continued that Kristian had gone to Nebraska, where there were men from Denmark. That's how it worked; newcomers sought out fellow countrymen. His employer at a creamery sent him to classes at Dana College to learn to speak, read, and write English. Margrethe, then a teenager, read his letters again and again, each time more determined she would go to America. In one letter, Kristian encouraged her and that was that. Still, it was with false bravado she left her dear family and homeland in late 1916. She brushed away the dread telling her she might never see them again.

Her mind lingered on the chain of events. She had become engaged to Hans Vesen, who then left for California and now requested that Margrethe join him and be married.

"You should not go to him," *Far* cautioned. "He showed up in the village but never said anything about where he came from. When he apprenticed in my cartwright business, he made the wrong size wheel for a customer. And he has a reputation for being too fond of alcohol."

"I've not seen that," Margrethe replied.

"Does he have a job?" *Far* inquired.

"In a fish cannery. They package sardines and pickled herring and they make lutefisk." Margrethe pinched her nose. She liked all these fish but not the smell.

Mor wrung her hands in her apron. "You should not travel alone. It's neither safe nor proper."

"I can take care of myself," Margrethe argued.

At twenty-one, she had no qualms about going alone. Well, maybe a few. She'd never been away from Aarre. She would miss village life, especially the blacksmith shop that *Bedstefar* Kristian once operated. As children, she and Dagmar loved spending time watching their grandfather work. They were cautious around the open fire, and played with the bellows when *Bedstefar* didn't need it. They huddled in a corner when those huge workhorses clomped in to be shod. *Bedstefar* died two years ago, well into his nineties, but not before building an immigrant trunk for Margrethe. The gleaming hammered tin design had bentwood straps and a rounded lid. Her eyes filled with tears whenever she looked at it. Nothing in the trunk had as much importance as the vessel itself.

As luck would have it, the problem was solved. Marinus Madsen had returned to Denmark to visit family. Margrethe would travel with him on his return to California.

Mor sighed with relief. "We have known Marinus since he was a child. You will be safe with him."

Far added, "He's a good man with a steady trade. Everyone needs shoes."

Margrethe barely knew Marinus but she felt better about having an escort. The trip from Aarre to their destination would be many weeks at sea and then across the vast United States, through cities and towns; tunnels and valleys; crossing rivers, prairies and mountains, to Los Angeles, where she would join Hans. They planned one stop, in South Dakota, to visit Kristian (Chris, as he now called himself), where he was a farmer, like his father and brother in the old country. He had never studied law. He had a new bride, Clara Hansen, American born, who spoke Danish.

Aboard ship, Marinus was a patient escort, a perfect gentleman, a quiet man, not given to small talk. Often there were long silences and they each sought the company of other passengers. Sometimes she and Marinus read books together, side by side in deck chairs, wrapped in blankets, as the crossing in December was windy and bone-chilling. Marinus had a tome about the American Civil War and she'd brought a collection of Hans Christian Andersen tales.

One morning, Marinus said, "To pass the time I will teach you to play poker."

Margrethe raised her eyebrows. "Gambling?"

"No, no. At home we play for only pennies."

When she beat him after three games, Marinus offered a sneaky smile. "Did you let me win?" Margrethe asked.

He smiled and handed her the shuffled cards. "Your deal."

Later, Marinus fell asleep in a deck chair next to Margrethe. He slept quietly, unlike Hans, who once fell asleep at a picnic and snored like Thor, the god of thunder. Margrethe had taken a walk to get away from the noise.

She glanced at Marinus. He was handsome, fairly tall, and slender, with pale blue eyes and dark hair with a strand or more of gray at the temples. He availed himself daily of the barber aboard who offered shaves and haircuts. Marinus's fingers were long, the nails neatly trimmed. Hans was red-haired, with dark blue eyes, stocky, and not much taller than Margrethe. His hands were rough, callused. Margrethe did not think him handsome, but his face was friendly and she liked his sense of humor. She blushed at the idea of sleeping with Hans, or any man, for that matter. Still, she couldn't help watching Marinus sleep.

Stop, her mind scolded. Why am I comparing them as if they are rivals? I need a walk to clear my mind.

She strolled to the ship's rail. She had no trouble with seasickness, but from the day they left Aarre, she felt home-sick. She missed her siblings, her loving *mor* and even *Far*'s patriarchal sternness. Mostly, she missed Dagmar, her mirror image, with whom she'd been born and spent the most time, awake at play, and asleep cuddled like spoons in a cutlery drawer.

Marinus had explained about Miss Liberty in New York City harbor, but Margrethe had not expected the giddi-ness she felt when first she glimpsed the welcoming statue. The closer the ship came, the more she thought she would swoon. Marinus laughed and held her hands to keep them from trembling. His hands were warm and smooth, like the leather he worked with daily. He stood behind her to ward off the cold wind, and then opened his overcoat and wrapped it around her. She enjoyed the feel of them being cocooned. But was it proper?

"We will come closer to her at Ellis Island," Marinus said. "Then you will see how truly big she is."

"And look at the buildings. They reach the clouds."

"Skyscrapers."

"Skyscrapers," Margrethe repeated, a new American word.

When they disembarked, Marinus led her to a bench. He often mixed English with Danish but she understood the gist of what he meant. "Watch our bags and I will find your trunk. It will take a while. Look at the line. You stay here; don't move *lille peega*. Don't talk to anyone. There are shysters and pickpockets about."

She had been called *lille peega* many times, little girl, but when it came from her father, it had usually been a scolding tone. Coming from Marinus, it sounded like an endearment. And here, in this big world, she surely felt little. What would she do if she had come alone? Thank God for Marinus.

People scurried about in a melody of languages and chaos, yelling, shoving, laughing, coughing, sneezing. Babies cried, children chased each other, carriages and carts and automobiles dodged one another. Horses snorted and plopped steaming manure on the ground. Feral dogs and cats skulked about. A woman who looked Slavic perched next to Margrethe and nursed an infant, her bosom barely covered. The baby's diaper needed changing. A toddler clutched the mother's skirt and a rag doll. The girl needed changing, too, bottom to top. There wasn't a person in sight who didn't look bedraggled, tired, and dirty. When she and Marinus arrived in South Dakota they would bathe, shampoo their hair, and wash and iron their clothing. That day couldn't come soon enough.

Margrethe smelled the salty ocean, dead fish, smoke, body odor, even her own, food, gasoline or kerosene, mildew, sewage, urine, and a mix of unidentified odors. Trash lay

238

strewn in corners, with rats digging into the piles. An enormous man strolled toward her with a cart offering "Hot Dogs." The piece of meat wrapped in bread looked tempting, and she was hungry, but she shook her head at the man. Then a mangy mutt bounced into the air and grabbed the man's hot dog in its mouth and ate it in one bite.

Margrethe laughed and looked in the direction Marinus had gone, eager for his return. It occurred to her that she could not recall the last time she'd thought about Hans. He was still far away. Weary, her head nodded but she should not sleep; her job was to watch their bags, and wait for Marinus.

She had no pocket watch to gauge the time, but then, at long last, there he came, hauling her precious trunk by the leather handle, its four wheels bumping over the rough terrain. The scene brought tears to her eyes and, once again, Marinus held her hand to comfort her. She could not recall Hans ever doing that.

Because Marinus spoke English and was a citizen, he helped Margrethe through the emigration process at Ellis Island, translating the questions thrown at her: Name, age, nationality, have you been in prison or the poorhouse, who paid your fare, are you married, do you have any skills, do you have a job at your destination, how much money do you have?

Margrethe had savings from caring for an elderly woman. Marinus helped her exchange Danish money for American dollars, and taught her the value of items so she wouldn't overpay. He guided them to the train station, from where they would travel west. At each stop along the way, Marinus bought newspapers for himself and women's magazines for her. He read every word of his papers, translated stories that might interest her, and explained the comic strips. She didn't understand some of the humor.

Paging through a magazine, looking at clothing and hair styles, she asked, "What is this word?"

"It says her suit is smart. It means stylish, fashionable."

New words again. Margrethe glanced at her travel-worn gray wool dress. The trip had taken a toll; she looked frumpy. She would need to be stylish now, and do something with her hair. Instead of the girlish braids that crowned her head, maybe the Gibson Girl look in the magazines.

Oh, and my shoes, Margrethe thought. She'd packed her old wooden *skos* in her trunk, and these traveling shoes were not fit to be seen. She tucked her feet under the seat so Marinus wouldn't notice.

Probably he already had. After all this time his suit and shirt and tie were wrinkled but he stilled looked well-groomed. He carried a tin of polish and had shined his ankle-high brogans along the way. She would ask him where to buy new shoes.

She fretted aloud, "There's so much I don't know, so much to learn."

"All in due time, *lille* one." Marinus stared at her, smiling.

On the day they parted company, Marinus said, "The young man will be with you in Los Angeles, the City of Angels. You will be fine." He had not mentioned Hans until now. He'd been gloomy and quieter than usual the past two days. Margrethe didn't mind; she, too, felt irritable, her nerves frayed like a skein of yarn clawed at by a kitten.

Marinus leaned over and kissed her forehead and then looked into her eyes. Flustered, and through her fears,

Margrethe summoned a smile for the man who had become more familiar to her than Hans. She had spent more time with Marinus than she ever had with Hans. She had already thanked Marinus for his help many times, but she thanked him again, and then, without thinking about what was proper, she tip-toed and kissed his cheek.

"*Farvel,*" she said, just above a whisper. Then she turned and walked away, tears in her eyes and anxiety churning her bones.

Visalia, California, 17 January, 1917

Visalia, 17 January 1917*

Dear Sister:

First of all, best wishes to you on your birthday. I don't know if this will arrive in time, but the thought is the best. Yes, you no doubt have heard what happened in Los Angeles. I could not feel at home there. Yes, dear sister, I can best tell you about it. I do not know how it came about that I started to care for Marinus, but it happened nevertheless against my will. The first time I recognized something in this way was a day on board ship. I was totally surprised because I thought I cared as much for Hans as could be possible. I thought of not seeing Marinus the following day, but there was nothing immoral in wanting to see him and I thought the feeling was probably just on my part. Yes, dear Hanne, I wish you could have seen him when I told him there was a man waiting for me. I thought he knew it, but he had no idea. He became so disappointed, but only said what would have been better if he had not spoken. "God's will, dear Margrethe, will see that it will be the best for both of us." But, Hanne, you can imagine it was hard for me see his dear face so unhappy, dark and gloomy. And before we parted he said that if it did not go well for me in Los Angeles, if I would then promise to come to him. He asked if I could come to Reedley to his brother's for Christmas. He could not stand to think that it was the last time he would see me without knowing that I had arrived safely at my destination. We parted the night before I arrived in Los Angeles. How I felt when I said goodbye to him that evening only God knew. It was much, much worse than when I said farewell to those at home. But fate looked upon us. We should be together after all. Hans Vasen was so cold towards me. I became more puzzled and unhappy than ever and the result was a break between us. He said straight out that he cared much more for many others than he had ever cared for me, but they had not cared for him. Finally, he said he thought he was a very bad fellow.

I wrote immediately to Marinus and told him everything and received the answer, "Come as soon as you can." He thought I could be there Thursday or Friday, but I could not come before Saturday. It took longer for the mail than we expected and he did not receive the card which announced my Saturday arrival until two days after I was supposed to come. He became so concerned something had happened to me that he left for Los Angeles on Saturday to get me and so we passed by each other. And there was a freight train derailed in a tunnel, so they were delayed there for a day, so he first came home the night between the first and second Christmas day. I did not know he had come home until the morning when I got up. I was alone there together with three of his sister-in-law's brothers, all very bright young men. And dear sister, what a welcome I got. Jens Madsen, his brother, together with one of his wife's (Maren) brothers, were at the station to see if I should be there. When Maren saw me she could not believe it was me. She exclaimed, "No, is that Margrethe? Now we can rightly celebrate Christmas all together." The four of us celebrated Christmas Eve alone, but otherwise it was a nice time.

Now I am going to work with an American family. I came there three days ago, Monday. Marinus did not want me to go, but I was afraid that I would not learn the language otherwise, but it is a hard school. I must admit that Marinus knew that and for that reason he did not want me to work, but if others can do it, so can I. The people are nice, but the lady does not have the right way of teaching the language, but we will see. I earn $15 a month to begin with. There is only one child, a small boy four-years-old. It is not far from where Marinus works. Otherwise there are only two Danish families here in town. It is a very pretty town, but about that another time. If you can, get a few words written to me. Many greetings and birthday congratulations to you from Marinus, but mostly from your little sister, Margrethe. Live well and say hello to the pastor and the people at home. It is cold here.

*actual letter, unedited from original FOOTNOTE

Margrethe laid aside her pen and let the ink dry on the pages. Her parents would be pleased with the outcome of Marinus. They had been right about Hans. He himself said he was a bad fellow. He had used a vulgarity, which Margrethe did not include in her letter. As for his promise to send money for her voyage, it never appeared. *Far* had purchased the ticket from his own wallet.

The couple would wed in May and settle in Reedley. Marinus would open a shoe repair shop and sell men's and boy's shoes. As *Far* had said, everyone needs shoes.

Margrethe wondered now if she had truly loved Hans. Or had she seen him as her ticket to America? Which, as it turned out, he hadn't provided. And when Hans broke off with her, he spoke of caring for others more than her. She knew his first interest was Dagmar, but it was an unrequited attraction so he courted Margrethe. And what if Hans had not broken off with her? Would she have married him, despite her strong feelings for Marinus, and his for her? What if there had been no Marinus to go to? She'd have had to fend for herself, a farm girl, alone in an immense city, among strangers, with no job, and she didn't speak English.

Recalling how bewildered she'd been back then, she took a deep breath. She had no regret. Her dream came true; she was in America. And she'd found true love. Of that she felt certain. They couldn't be happier. Well, perhaps they could; if God's plan included a handful of children, that would be an added blessing.

Reedley, California, May 1917

Margrethe wore the white bridal dress she had made from crepe de chine. Marinus found white shoes for her. Mor sent sheer white stockings ordered from Copenhagen. Dagmar had crocheted a white headpiece with a net veil. A white satin ribbon held together the bride's bouquet of red California poppies. Marinus's brother and his wife were Best Man and Maid of Honor. The Scandinavian Lutheran Church pews held only a few guests: Marinus's relatives, four of his friends, and Margrethe's employers.

Do thee, Margrethe....

I do....

Do thee, Marinus....

I do....

With this ring, I thee wed....

I pronounce you man and wife.

You may kiss the bride.

[section break]

Reedley, California, 1917-1948

Margrethe Americanized her name to Margaret. During the first years of their marriage, Marinus lost personal customers due to a leather shortage created by The Great War in Europe. But he gained a government contract to provide shoes for the military forces. They made do with a steady income.

The couple had four children: Anna Cecilla, Elmer Ernest, and twins, Ruth Margaret and Alice Marie. Busy raising a family, they never returned to Denmark, but in 1938 they journeyed to South Dakota to visit Margaret's brother, Chris, and his family of seven children. Farming had not suited him; he worked at the local creamery making butter. As customary, folks from the old country, relatives, friends, and sometimes strangers, came day and night to join the happy gatherings.

Margaret and Marinus had only thirty years together. They died at a young age, Marinus in 1947, and Margaret in 1948.

Margrethe's letter eventually found its way to her children, a handwritten record of their parents' love story in their mother's words and native language.

Dear Sister....

And their father's optimistic hope, *"God's will, dear Margrethe, will see that it will be the best for both of us."*

The Dance of Destiny

by Jasmine Tritten

For the eight months Jim and I had dated, the serious subject of a future together never came up. Our jobs kept us busy. Still, whenever I glanced at Jim, I got butterflies in my stomach. *I wonder if men ever get butterflies in their stomachs.*

One evening in the year 1990, during a social function at the Naval Postgraduate School in Monterey, California, an attractive lady approached my friend Jim and me.

"You two are such a nice-looking couple. Would you like to housesit our beautiful home in Carmel Valley while my husband and I move to Panama for two years?"

My mouth fell open, but words did not come out. Mainly because of the brief encounter with this woman named Mary. Her husband did some Navy-related work with Jim. *Still, how could she trust us? She must be desperate to find somebody.* I turned my head towards Jim, and wondered what he thought. He looked at me, and twisted his mustache with a question mark written all over his face.

Of course, we look good together because we are in love. It sounds intriguing, and I am crazy about Jim. But we are neither married nor engaged. What are we going to do?

"What do you think?" Jim asked me.

Whatever he decided, I planned to follow. I was so in love with this guy I could hardly see straight. However, one suggestion,

"Let's go to check out the house and then make a decision."

It might be a dump.

Off we went the next day with Mary. We walked from the car up to the house.

"Oh, what a heavenly place. Those mountains, and look down the valley, all those trees Jim," I said in a bubbly voice. Then we stepped into the divine space. My eyes moved from the tall, beamed ceiling in the living room to the enormous fireplace. Each of the three bedrooms had a view of bushes or trees, soothing to my soul. As we stood on the spacious deck after having checked out every inch of the house, I grabbed Jim's arm,

"This is like a dream come true."

Mary turned towards us and said, "What I really would like is for somebody reliable to take care of our house for the full two years we are away. Somebody we can trust and who will pay the rent each month."

"We understand," I responded. *To live in this house is a big undertaking and responsibility for two people who are not an item yet. We don't even know if we can live together.*

"Your house is beautiful. We love it, but we must first discuss how we can make it possible," I said to her and smiled.

After the tour of Mary's house, we stood under a tall tree overlooking the valley. In awe over the beauty surrounding me, I walked over to Jim. He put his arms around me, peered straight into my eyes, and said,

"We haven't discussed our relationship yet. Here is such a wonderful opportunity for us to find out if we get along in daily life. How about we move into this house together?"

My heart throbbed in my chest. All I thought about was being with this man any way possible.

"I would love that," I quickly replied and drowned in his warm hazel-brown eyes. From his six-foot, two-inches stature, he reached down and kissed my lips. Hugging Jim felt like coming home. *If only I could stay in his embrace forever and never let go.*

"I'll take a chance with you," I whispered in his ear.

Things I liked about Jim: Everything. So handsome. A real gentleman. Nurturing. Caring and thoughtful. Supportive. I loved his romantic Hungarian side. He always turned me on. His deep voice sang in my ears. His intelligence and sense of humor hit many spots in me. Full of ideas. Loyal. Dependable. Thorough. A creative thinker. Unique. Prompt, never late. I treasured that.

I love him, and I want our relationship to flourish.

The moment I think back to how we met, I smile inside. A wonderful couple arranged for us to meet at their home in the Carmel Valley. The Norwegian wife happened to be my friend. Her husband worked with Jim at the Naval Postgraduate School in Monterey. They set us up.

Brit called me one day and said, "Jasmine, you've got to meet this awesome guy who is going to live in our house for six months while we go to Norway. Robert will show him the house Sunday morning. So come over for breakfast."

"Where does he come from?" I questioned.

"He just separated from his wife," she told me.

"Oooops!" I went. Red lights flared up all around me.

Deep inside, I knew never to become involved with anybody who had just come out of a relationship. Except curiosity struck. *To meet someone for breakfast can't hurt.*

"Okay, I would like to come over and meet him," I said to Brit.

The Sunday breakfast meal turned out a bit awkward. Brit's husband Robert showed Jim the house and what he had to do, and Jim had no idea why I was there. But I checked him out while we ate and liked what I saw. Later in the day, Brit called me,

"Jasmine, is it okay to give Jim your phone number? He asked for it!"

That can't hurt, just a number, I thought.

"Sure, that's fine," I told her.

Later in the afternoon, Jim phoned.

"Would you like to hike in the mountains next Sunday?" he asked.

It sounds safe. His soothing voice hypnotized me.

"I'd like that," I responded.

We trudged mountain trails around the Monterey Peninsula for five consecutive Sundays before we even held hands. Nature spoke to us both. I felt comfortable walking next to him, talking, learning about his life in the U.S. Navy and as a professor at the Naval Postgraduate School.

Most of what I wanted in a man I wrote on a list two weeks before I met Jim. Then it materialized in front of my eyes. He turned out to be the man for me. To make sure, I checked our birth charts through astrology. Yep, excellent compatibility. Maybe even soul mates. Still, we had stumbling blocks to process.

The day after our tour of the house, I called Mary on the phone.

"We have decided to take you up on your offer, and promise to take care of your house until you return. Just let us know when you'll be ready to leave," I told her.

Within a month, we moved into the furnished dream house on the hillside in Carmel Valley. Green light so far. Two cats that belonged to Jim came with us. What a blessing I loved cats, because I would be left out in the cold with no Jim if I did not.

At first, when we met, he showed me the place where he lived, and I asked him, "What are those two lumps under the cover in the middle of the king-size bed?"

"One is my cat, Dexter. The other his brother Nevil," he replied.

Of course, it might as well have been a duck and a chicken. But I believed every word he said. In my life, I had never met a man who played the classical radio station all day long for his cats, and who wanted them to listen to soothing music while he went to work. One primary reason for which I liked Jim. *Possibly he would spoil me, too.*

Jim cared enormously about his cats, the two brothers. Nobody fancied felines more than him. One cat, Dexter, rested on his shoulders for hours while he sat and worked on his computer.

"I would like a cat too," I said to him one day. Not only did I find Shakti at the shelter with yellow eyes buried in short, thick, greyish fur; in addition, a Siamese with blue eyes I named Ninotchka after my favorite Greta Garbo movie. Everybody got along well. Jim always said, "We can never have enough cats."

So, we lived in a cat house like Ernest Hemmingway in Key West.

"Can we come and stay with you for a couple of days?" became a standard line from our family members after we moved into the Carmel Valley house. Nobody believed our fantastic place and blissful situation. The love Jim and I had for each other grew stronger everyday as layers from the past peeled off and vanished. Months went by.

Thanksgiving came around. Most family members lived far away, either in Denmark, Texas, New York, or Florida, so we decided to celebrate the special day with friends nearby. For the occasion, we joined a close colleague of Jim's in his home in Monterey together with his family. This unusual couple happened to argue regularly and were known as the "Battling Bickersons." Except during our visit, they behaved exceptionally well. Lucky for us!

White lit candles in silver candlesticks glowed on the long, carved wooden table and cast shadows on the white tablecloth. At each end stood vases with purple and white flowers. The aroma of an enormous golden-brown turkey, stuffing, mashed potatoes, green beans, and cranberry sauce reached my nostrils. Pumpkin pie for dessert. Enough food for an army. Bottles of red and white wine with numerous glasses filled the rest of the exquisite table. A feast for the eyes soon became a feast for the belly.

Apart from Jim, I knew only his friend and wife. Nothing mattered to me except being next to my Jim. We consumed the tasty food, drank the delicious wine, and talked for hours in delightful company. At the end of the festive meal, Jim raised his glass and gave an appropriate Thanksgiving speech.

Then he asked every single individual around the table, "Tell me, what you are thankful for on this Thanksgiving Day?"

Each person gave a different answer, and when my turn came, I held up my glass, stared into his smiling eyes, and said, "I'm thankful for you, Jim!"

For some reason, the response must have been correct because after everyone expressed their gratitude, Jim pulled himself up from his chair and lifted his glass,

"I have met the most beautiful girl in the universe with blue eyes and blonde hair from my favorite country, Denmark." Then he looked intensely into my eyes and, with a mellow voice, said,

"I am so thankful for you, Jasmine. Will you marry me?"

A profound silence followed for an entire minute. One could hear a needle drop to the floor. *Is he joking?* I wondered. A flush of adrenaline tingled through my body.

"Aren't you going to answer him? Say yes! Say yes!" Our friends cheered and encouraged me to respond.

At that instant, I remembered Cher from the movie *Moonstruck* we viewed recently. Nicolas Cage proposed to her in a restaurant, and she told him to get on his knees first.

Warmth radiated in my chest, and I replied, "Of course, I will marry you, but first, please kneel before I accept."

Everybody in the room laughed in surprise.

Jim fell to his knees, then looked up at me with his warm brown eyes, pleading, "Jasmine, will you marry me?"

How could I resist.

"Of course, I'll marry you. Yes, yes, yes," I answered my prince in a light, bubbly voice. What else could I do? I loved that man with all my heart.

The moment he got himself back up, we kissed and hugged for a long time. The sounds of people clapping and hollering filled my ears, and tears of joy overflowed my eyes—an engagement to remember forever.

One without a ring on my finger because Jim proposed at the spur of the moment. For that, I remained grateful.

"I look forward to growing old with you," he said.

I answered, "What about all the wrinkles and gray hair?"

He replied, "I won't see them."

What more could I ask for in a soon-to-be husband?

A couple days after our engagement, we sat around the fireplace in the evening and talked about plans for Christmas coming up the following month.

Jim suddenly jumped up from the couch, "How about we get married the week after Christmas. Our families are flying out here anyway for the holidays. That way, they don't have to come back a second time for our wedding."

"Brilliant idea, except we only have one month to prepare," I said and threw my hands up in the air. Often, Jim came up with superb ideas, which I appreciated, but this one sounded impossible.

"We can do it," he said with a wide grin and embraced me. "We can have the wedding ceremony in the chapel at the Naval Postgraduate School. It will be wonderful," he continued.

For a moment, I melted, then replied, "That's easy for you to say. Naturally, I want to marry you. Except for all the arrangements we'll have to make in a hurry, and guess who must make most of them? I don't know if I can do it all. Besides, I need a dress and to have a ring designed."

The thought of a big wedding overwhelmed me. During that time, I studied for a degree in interior design at the Monterey Peninsula College and did therapeutic massage for a chiropractor. Professor Jim worked and traveled constantly.

After a bear hug, he lifted me from the ground and swirled me around.

"No need for a large wedding, since it's the second time for both of us. How about fifty people?" he suggested in a calm voice and set me down.

"Okay, I can probably manage that," I said and released an appreciative sigh. Everything changed in a moment from being impossible to fantastic, and we danced in circles around the living room. No matter how difficult any situation seemed at first, Jim always came up with a magical solution. The key to a lasting relationship.

"My wedding ring!" I yelled.

"Calm down," he said in his soothing voice. "I bought a diamond in Washington D.C. last week. We'll have Robert and Brit's amazing jeweler in Carmel make it into an artsy gold ring for you with an intricate design. All I need is a plain gold band." I kissed his cheek.

During our ceremony, Jim put on my finger a gorgeous creation of a wedding band. For sure, it made up for the one I did not receive when he proposed to me. The golden treasure with the diamond stretched from my knuckle to the first joint of my ring finger, for sure a statement of this man's love for me. At the same time, a "handy" defense weapon.

My wedding dress? In a bridal shop in Monterey, I found a dress in my favorite color, lavender, with a high neck, long sleeves, slightly pleated, mid-calf long. Fit in the waist. The chiffon fabric flowed like a dream. A lavender hat decorated with tiny pearl beads and a short veil in the back made the outfit complete, together with matching shoes.

We made it. Within one month, a whirlwind of a fabulous wedding got planned. Everything I did with this man of mine always worked out.

Except for when we sat in the chapel and waited for the groom. He did not show up.

"Where's Jim? What's happened to him?"

We waited and waited. Everybody worried but me. *I know he will show up because he is my soul mate and we are meant to be together.*

Then at long last, he rushed through the door in his tuxedo, up the middle aisle towards the altar. His hair looked shorter. The barber arrived late, and who but Jim would cut his hair right before a wedding.

In the middle of the ceremony, a peculiar sound came from the sides of the chapel. Our wedding guests peeked through the windows and spotted peacocks pecking at the glass from the outside. A positive omen for our marriage since these colorful birds were my favorites. Usually, they roamed the grounds.

By the time we said our vows, and "I do," "I will," "Yes," I felt blessed. Because I was crazy about my new husband in his tuxedo, I did not know which foot to stand on. Following the tender wedding kiss and the congratulations, Jim announced, "Let's all go to the Carmel Valley house for the reception."

Family and friends joined us in celebrating the joyous event. My son Chris surprised us with a fantastic speech I will always remember. After socializing, drinking champagne and cutting the cake with Jim's U.S. Navy officer's sword, he and I ended up outside the house on the large deck, our favorite spot. We glanced across the Carmel Valley to the mountains in the distance, until Jim turned around, put his arms around me, kissed my cheek affectionately and said,

"I'm so grateful you are in my life and that we moved into this beautiful place together. It must be destiny. I look forward to each moment with you every day forever."

It's a Love Story, Afterall

by Jenna Wilson

Ever since my teen years, I was the Valentine's Day version of Ebenezer Scrooge—I *hated* love stories. I mumbled and grumbled my way through them, always celebrating February 15th as "Discount Chocolate Day" instead. I thought the whole concept of a "love story" was unreasonable, and that belief only grew stronger over time.

When I was teaching eighth grade at a small school in a larger metropolitan area, I was tasked with preparing my students, who had the same thirty classmates since preschool, for their experiences in high schools with about two thousand students each. I once asked my class what they were most excited about, and one girl raised her hand. When I called on her, she first responded with a deep sigh. She then leaned forward and placed her chin in the palm of her hand with her elbow resting on the desk and raised her eyes skyward while literally twirling her hair. The only bit missing from this scene of stereotypical adolescent femininity was a pop of bubble gum at her lips. Once in position, she said to me: "I just can't wait to have a real, true love story. You know, like *The Fault in Our Stars."*

Dear God, if *that* is what this child was hoping for, I didn't know if I should roll my eyes or send her to a social worker. It's a beautifully written, heart-wrenching tearjerker for sure, but it's the last thing I'd call "a real, true love story."

I completely understand why she was swooning. It's the same reason millions of people each year buy romance movies and novels—both the wholesome kind and their more, ahem, *provocative* counterparts. These stories are fun to read. They give our hearts something to long for. They show a world where meeting a partner is more than just a swipe on a dating app. They're absolutely dreamy.

And that's why I hated them.

I even had a scripted rant to prove it:

1. 1.   They're rife with terrible aphorisms and empty advice about how to live life as a functioning adult.

2. 2.   The plots are completely unreasonable. A couple changes their mind about divorce after watching their daughter fall in love, or a therapist and her patient with cancer come together after he survives, or two dying kids live every possible life dream before their lives end. Come on, right?

3. 3.   For teens and adults like my student who are wondering how love happens and what it means, these books offer nothing at best, and problematic perspectives at worst. I can't count how many young adult novels out there show abusive relationships as sexy.

4. 4.   And finally, what I hate the most about romance—the impossibility of the decision making. They tell us that you "just know" when you've found "the one." They tell us that "it happens when you least expect it." Love stories are always rooted in these insanely emotional experiences, as if whatever they're processing initially (cancer, divorce, grief) isn't enough. But even through mind-altering, life changing challenges, two people see each other and have a date and *just know*.

Right.

I've always told my students that the love story you want is two people brushing their teeth at the same sink every day. The magic of these movies and books, it's not real. Too many people want a wedding but not a marriage, a ring but not a partner. I firmly believed that for most of my life, and no one could change my mind. At least, that's what I thought until I actually lived one.

It all started when I met Joe in January of 2010. Before you ask, the answer is no—Joe is not my husband or a protagonist in my love story. He is a very important character, though. Joe and I used to joke that we had zero percent of each other one day and one hundred percent the next. I was in community college, and I worked in a co-op program with our local Veteran's Affairs hospital. I was the student co-op assistant in payroll, and he held the same role in human resources. I'd had that job for six months, but I never realized Joe worked right down the hallway. One day they had him cover the phone in the payroll office, and there he was—a rare coworker who *wasn't* at least a decade older than me. I was immediately interested in possibly having lunch with someone who had stories about things besides kids and paying bills, but I didn't get the chance to talk to him right away. But when that semester's classes began a few days later, I found him in my literature class and my theater class. That semester we saw each other every day, all day between work and school, and we shared the stage in a production of a raunchy southern comedy with jokes about miscarriage and religion that certainly have not aged well. I played his mother.

It's very possible that our friendship was born from nothing more than residual stage chemistry, but it was born just the same. We discovered we were both passionate writers, beatniks at heart, and at the time, in love with people who were wrong for us. We told each other that, but neither of us listened.

Over the next few years, Joe and I sort of danced through the mess of our lives with each other in pocket. We rarely lived in the same place, but we talked at least weekly and made spur of the moment road trips when the other was having a tough time.

I remember when I was student teaching and dating a boyfriend who I was at least willing to marry, but definitely not meant to be with. Joe called me just to see how my week was going and I answered the phone in tears.

"We had a fight," I told him. "We always fight just before there's something important in my life. That way he doesn't have to go."

"What's important this time?" he asked.

"It's stupid," I responded, rolling my eyes at myself.

"If it's important to you, Jenna, then it isn't stupid. And if it's important to you, then it's important to me."

With a hesitant smile, I told Joe that my students were doing a play. I really wanted to go support them, but I didn't want to go alone.

"What time does it start?" he asked. And even though the play was that same evening and Joe lived forty-five minutes away, he jumped in his car and made it in time to take me out for dinner beforehand, too.

My friend Joe was always there for me because that was the kind of kind soul he was. I tried to return the favor and be there for him always, too. I brought him booze and snacks when he learned his girlfriend cheated, and I let him talk through all of his first-dates to offer a female perspective. I still remember when I met the girl he ended up proposing to. At the last second as we entered the room, he told me I had to pretend he was a Kesha fan. Throughout the whole lunch, I tried inserting Kesha song titles into conversation as naturally as possible. Joe stepped on my foot under the table more than once, but he laughed about it for months afterwards. A few months later, when he met my next fling, Jake, Joe told me I had to dump him immediately because he didn't wash his hands for a full twenty seconds.

Joe was always in my life. He wasn't my very best friend, really, but he was constant and important. Even if we didn't talk for weeks, I knew I could call him any time and he would be there.

Joe and I were never in love.

It would make a great story if we had been, but real life doesn't work the way those movies work. Joe and I understood each other as writers and actors. We were both hopeless romantics, too, but I was a bit more cynical. I didn't believe in chance encounters or passion between strangers like Joe did.

In the summer of 2012, I told Joe I'd given up on love. I'd just wait for a guy to maybe call me like in that song and then I'd marry him. That same day, a guy handing out cheese samples at the grocery store chatted me up, gave me his number, and quoted the song. Joe was convinced he was my soulmate. He wasn't, of course, though we remain friends. But that didn't matter to Joe. He called me every day for a week to ask me if I'd kissed the cheese guy yet. He just believed that coincidence had to matter.

Love stories made my eyes roll—well, they made his eyes roll, too, but with more of a smile. His perspective on life was never optimistic, but it could be wholesome and healing in a way that was contagious. I know Joe helped me heal and grow. I like to think I helped him, too. But not enough.

In August of 2014, Joe took his own life.

I could write thousands of pages about the hurt and the loss and the grief of the moment I learned he was gone. I thought Joe was my constant. I thought he would always be there. When I learned that the darkness I always knew he carried had overwhelmed him to that point, and I wasn't there to help him carry it, my darkness began to overwhelm me, too. Joe's suicide also came less than a year after the suicide of my closest friend. Life began to swell around me, trapping me in place, making me feel like a rowboat with a leak navigating the choppy, dark waters of grief.

I remember Joe's funeral in bits and pieces. There were boxes of tissues everywhere, staged conveniently next to posters filled with Joe's smiles over the years. I remember seeing a picture of his chubby years and smiling, then feeling gutted by a picture from the last time I saw him. The air was surprisingly unscented for how many flowers I saw. The crowd was decades younger than the average funeral, and for every clear, somber face, there were two more with red cheeks and puffy eyes. Flowing through this room was a river of grief – the ocean that had kept me trapped had been granted movement, and no one could stay anchored for long.

Joe's family requested for people to come prepared to share stories about Joe, and that made so much sense. Joe was made up of stories and poems sewn together by a string of uncertainty, and the most beautiful way to honor his memory was to speak them into the room. I remember clutching three pages of moments with Joe and waiting for his family to open the floor to those who wanted to share. When they finally did, I knew I didn't deserve to go first, so I waited.

But no one spoke.

The silence crashed into the room. Joe's father was reaching, asking if *anyone* had *anything* to say, and he sounded like he was on the verge of ending the service. All I could think was if any person in that room was in the casket, and Joe were sitting in a seat, he wouldn't think twice to stand and say something so magical that every mourning soul would forget, for just a second, that they weren't supposed to be happy.

So, I stood up.

To be completely honest, I've blacked out most of this memory. I was grieving so deeply that I couldn't even taste food or drinks, and my mind just couldn't hold on to all of those moments. But I know I held a microphone at the front of the room and made a lot of tearful statements and then sat back down.

Then someone else stood up, walked to the front of the room, and started talking. When I found the nerve to lift my eyes to see him, my first thought was, *Damn, he is cute,* followed closely by *Oh my God, Jenna. You're literally at Joe's funeral right now. You can't think things like that!* But Joe, through all of his heartbreak, remained a hopeless romantic—more Ginsberg than Kerouac, really, though he'd never admit it—and he was always trying to write my love story for me. I knew he'd chuckle at that first thought, and I settled into a bit of peace while I listened to the cute guy speak and those who followed.

After the service ended, I found myself at the front of the room saying goodbye to Joe in my own way, and that cute guy who'd spoken after me asked if I'd like a hug. It's funny, now, because I know he's not a hugger. I felt his arms wrap around me as my cheek rested on the button holding his collar to his shirt. His face was covered with this glorious beard—blond and brown together, a glaze of scruff across his chin and cheeks—and it lightly grazed my forehead. I folded my arms around his waist and felt my shoulders melt a little. I'd never felt so comfortable hugging a stranger.

"I'm Adam. You probably don't remember me," he whispered, his voice a bit of a solemn croak. "But I think we met one year at Joe's New Year's Eve party."

I knew immediately that he was wrong. I'd been to Joe's apartment on New Year's Eve before, but there was no way I could have met this beautiful bearded man who was holding me now and forgotten him. But I still answered with "Yeah, we might have," because it felt like what Joe would have told me to say. It was the thing to keep the cute guy—Adam—talking.

We stepped away from one another as Joe's brother approached. He looked almost exactly like Joe, and he was wearing Joe's clothes. He was the spitting image of the smiling kid in the payroll office that day four years before. It cut me off at the knees.

"Hey, are you guys going to the wake?" He asked, handing me a card with a picture of a poker game featuring Jesus, Joe with a halo, and some others.

"Oh, I don't know…" I started. I flipped the card over and found the address to be a restaurant about a half a mile from my apartment.

"You should go," Adam said. "I'll see you there."

So I went. I got there kind of early and ordered rice and beans because I didn't know what else to do. More people arrived slowly, then all at once, and I met so many people who knew Joe in different realms of his life that my grieving shifted. I wasn't lost anymore. Instead, I was floating alongside others who were floating, too. I reconnected with those we'd acted with, coworkers from his various jobs, family members I'd heard endless stories about, and Adam. Adam told me more about himself as we both wandered in and out of conversations. Adam, along with many others, shifted from "a person who knew Joe" to "a person I know."

When I needed to leave, I knew I had to say goodbye to Adam. I was exhausted to my core, and I just wanted to slip out of the restaurant and into my bed to cry until sleep took over. But Joe would have wanted me to have enough nerve to say goodbye to the cute guy, right? That's the only way it worked. I had zero interest in dating anyone, having recently ended a long-dead relationship before grief bled its way into my life. But I just had the sense that I needed to talk to the cute guy once more.

"Hey," I said, sidling up next to him in the brief moment he was between conversations with Joe's brother and other friends. "I'm heading out, and I wanted to say goodbye. And thank you for welcoming me, too."

Adam's eyes were hazy with grief and the echoes of the beers we all drank in Joe's honor as he looked towards me. He put out his arm and hugged me in that half-bodied way we hug the people we want to embrace but don't know well enough just yet.

"Hey, I want to keep in touch with you," he said. "You said you live in Bloomington?"

"Oh, no – not anymore. I live here now. Just a few blocks away, actually."

"Oh, that's good. Okay. Here, what's your phone number? I'll text you mine."

Suddenly I was in over my head. I started talking to this guy because I liked him and I knew Joe would have liked that, but now I needed Joe – my wingman, my backup, my brother – to tell me how to react when a cute guy asks for my number. I didn't know what to do. So, I did what reasonably made sense – I just listed the digits of my phone number. Just as I was feeling like a total fool for not having some cute, charming response, my phone buzzed in my hand.

"Well, I just texted you my name, but I spelled it wrong." Adam was looking at his phone screen, and when I glanced down, I saw the obvious typo. We both laughed, and I knew in that moment that I hadn't needed to be cute or charming. I just needed to be Jenna.

We had our first date after two weeks of constant texting whenever we were both awake. Adam worked third shift as a route diagrammer for a trucking company and I was teaching eighth grade English. He stayed up late and woke up early just to make sure we'd be able to talk more. I learned so much about him. We both loved camping. He was close with his family, and he was both a cat person and a dog person. We had the same taste in music, mostly, but there were a few bands I may have pretended to know better than I did. While I was wrapped in the clutches of absolute grief, I found my heart feeling lighter every time his name popped onto my phone's screen. I could feel Joe's smile every time.

It was clear Adam was different and our relationship was going to be different, and our first date sealed that for me. I was waiting and hoping and praying he would ask me out. When he finally did, I panicked. I didn't want to seem like some lame homebody who didn't make weekend plans (even though that's exactly who I was... and am). I told him I had dinner plans, but that I could see him after.

My roommate made sure I wasn't a liar and took me to dinner at that same restaurant where I'd exchanged phone numbers with Adam two weeks before. I sipped a margarita and tried using chips and guac to stop my stomach from rising into my throat. It barely worked. When it was time, I went to the bar where we agreed to meet and waited inside.

I was nervous. It had been, let's just say, a *very* long time since I'd had a first date, and this one didn't exactly feel conventional. I didn't know how to reconcile the aching chasm inside of my heart that Joe left behind with the fluttering, silly happiness of a new interest. But when Adam walked up to the door, he paused for a moment. He took a deep breath, his shoulders rising and falling, before he nodded his head.

I knew then he was feeling exactly what I was: a slurry of grief, confusion, nostalgia, and melancholy with all of the things we thought we weren't supposed to feel, too—hope, wonder, and anticipation.

Point four on my scripted list of reasons to detest love stories, and the one I hated the most, is the sentiment that "you just know." It's unrealistic, right? In these movies and books, one character sees another doing something so mediocre, like cleaning up a spill or filling in a crossword puzzle, and they suddenly "know" they'll commit their lives to that person? I refused to accept that that was possible. But in the moment that Adam walked in and nervously sat down in front of me, after watching him prepare himself for our date and talking to him constantly in the two previous weeks, something clicked in my mind and my heart. The thought arose before I could even register its significance: "I'm going to keep him forever."

I just knew.

For a long time, I rolled my eyes at myself when I thought about how clearly I *knew*. I hated this concept because I'd spent much of my life *thinking*. I thought I was going to marry both of my high school boyfriends. The first one is doing well. Last I heard he's not in jail anymore, so that's good. The second one is now happily married to someone else. I even dated a man about eight years older than me for a while in college, thinking he would make a great forever despite his inability to communicate feelings and his unwillingness to make room for me in his life. And I really, truly *thought* I would marry all of them.

I didn't realize the difference between thinking and knowing until I knew.

The beginning of my relationship with Adam was a curious cocktail of fun and sorrow. We had a lot of good times together, and our chemistry was undeniable. But we were both still grieving a huge loss, and grief doesn't just go away because another big, important feeling comes, too. While our relationship took root and worked to bloom through that darkness, we got to know each other and the serendipity surrounding our love.

One night at my apartment over take-out food and a few drinks, Adam told me a lot more about how he knew Joe. They became close in high school, best friends. They attended the same small, rural Illinois school about 12 miles from my own.

"I graduated high school and went to community college in town," he said.

"Wait – that's where I met Joe. When were you there?"

"I left in 2009, but Joe was still there for another year."

I laughed at the misalignment of it all. "I came in the fall of 2009. Right after you left."

Adam smiled, too, before bringing up the party he'd mentioned when we met at Joe's funeral.

"I thought I had met you at Joe's apartment on New Year's Eve, but it might not have been you." He took a thoughtful swig of his beer and continued. "I think that year was 2011?"

I blinked back amazement. "I think that was the year I went to his apartment on New Year's Eve, but left long before the party actually started. You must have come after me."

"That's just crazy," he said, shaking his head. "We might have met years ago if you hadn't had some other big party to attend, or if I'd been earlier."

"Yeah, just crazy," I said, not mentioning that I definitely didn't have another party to attend – I just went home to eat pizza with my roommate.

One night, in a sort of grief-induced masochistic nostalgia, I pulled out the DVD of the play Joe and I performed in together. This play is what truly solidified our friendship. We had the only serious scene in the entire thing, and we'd have been damned if we didn't make it Tony-Award-worthy. Every time we ran that show, Joe and I sat on the couch backstage in the dark and held hands while we tried to make ourselves cry. I remember the feeling so clearly - his hand lightly gripping mine, my mind replaying all of my life's saddest moments, and ultimately walking on stage with tears in my eyes and Joe at my side. It was an incredibly emotional experience for both of us. When the opening credits ended and the screen showed a wobbly, fuzzy view of our college stage, Adam laughed.

"No way!" He said around his smile.

"What?"

"I remember this play. I saw it twice."

I blinked at him. "Twice?"

"Yeah. It was good. Which one were you? I remember the mother was hilarious."

I shook my head, wondering if he'd even believe me. "I *was* the mother."

"Oh my God, this is hilarious. You know, I stopped to talk to Joe in the crowd after both of those plays, but I still somehow never met you."

"Yeah, and that really is wild because Joe and I typically walked out together. I guess you caught him up while I was with someone else."

All sorts of little moments like this popped into our conversations. Adam would try to describe something in one of Joe's apartments and I'd know what he meant before he finished the sentence. He would tell me a story about a bar Joe loved, and I'd tell him I went there with him, too.

For four years, I was closely connected with Joe and Joe was closely connected with Adam, but Adam and I repeatedly missed meeting each other by what felt like the blink of an eye. The cynic in me wanted to call it coincidence, the haphazard shape of early adulthood. But that simply can't be true. I never believed in divine intervention, but I have no doubt that Joe brought the two of us together to make sure we'd never be lonely, even without him.

One cold winter night, Adam was driving me home from dinner, and we stopped at the pharmacy to pick up my prescription. We'd only been together a few months, and we were still exploring one another, finding every squeaky stair and floorboard in each other's mind. We were talking about exes, and I had just finished telling him about the man I'd been dating before him.

"I mean, I think he's a good person, but we weren't a good couple. It just didn't feel like a forever kind of thing."

"I know what you mean," he said, starting the car in the dark November chill. "I've felt that before. When you just know it isn't the right thing for you."

"Yeah," I agreed. And the next words came before I even realized what I was saying. "But not like this. I've never felt anything like this, with you, before."

It was a scary moment. The split second that the words left my lips, I worried he may reject me. But that anxiety died as soon as it was born. Adam steered the car towards the exit of the Walgreens parking lot with one hand and reached the other to the right to grasp my fingers. His palms were calloused and warm, and he rubbed his thumb on the side of my hand as he said, "I never have, either."

He just knew, too.

And that certainty stayed with us. After six months together, I applied for a teaching job back in my home county, forty minutes from where I was currently working. I got it. After nine months together, Adam and I moved in with each other. A year and a half later we bought a house. We were doing all of the grown-up, being-in-love things— except for the marriage part.

Maybe it's my millennialism, but I strongly believed I should live with any partner before I committed to marriage, even when I knew that Adam was the person I'd want to spend the rest of my life with. My Roman Catholic family, for the most part, didn't love this decision, though they always supported me. More than two years after our untraditional meeting, we signed a mortgage agreement but not a marriage license. At that point, my left ring finger was starting to feel more naked than it ever had before. I didn't necessarily feel like I needed to be married, but I was so overwhelmed by everyone around me expecting us to get married and the lack of control I had over that, since I knew Adam would be the one to propose.

Adam and I talked about marriage, picked out rings, and even planned our ideal timeframe—an October 2017 wedding. But December 2016 rolled around, and we had nothing but figurative plans. I knew in my heart that Adam was my forever and he felt the same way. I didn't *want* to demand a ring to prove it, but I was frustrated by the societal boundaries on engagement. All I could do was wait.

But waiting wasn't working for me, so I attempted to nudge the process along. I spent many weekends trying to plan the perfect evening so he could propose. I suggested dinner dates at fancy restaurants, walks along beautiful lakes in state parks, weekend getaways to small rural wineries and big cities alike. We did a lot of these things and I truly enjoyed them, but the engagement never came. My nerves started running on edge and I began to obsess a bit over the idea of engagement, seeing proposable moments everywhere and noticing even more how many people I saw with wedding rings.

We'd been living in our new house for a month, and it felt like all the big opportunities had passed us. I didn't truly *want* a big engagement with all the fanfare, but for whatever reason, that was what I expected to happen. That's just *how* it happens, right? That's what the romance stories tell us, after all.

Thankfully, as always, my wonderful partner knew better.

I am a homebody. I made up pretend plans the night of our first date so Adam wouldn't think I was a homebody, but it turned out we both love a good home-cooked meal and a movie on the couch. These big events I was suggesting were fun but exhausting to both of us. Adam knew that wasn't the best way to start our forever.

One Saturday night, Adam suggested we go grocery shopping. "It's never busy on a Saturday night," he said. "We can make some burgers after."

When we came home with a trunk full of groceries, he told me to go unlock the door and he'd carry them in.

"I had a new key made for you," he said. "I know you like your house keys to have a design."

I grabbed the key he handed me. It was black with a little red heart and it said "HOME" across the top. It was paired with a keychain I struggled to read in the dark that said "The Wilsons." I gave him a quick kiss and said thank you before heading to unlock the door.

After that, time seemed to slow down, and I registered the rest of the moment in bits and pieces.

First, Adam laughed, which seemed odd. When I put the key into the knob, I stopped. *The Wilsons? That's not my last name.* I walked into the kitchen and turned the keychain over to find my husband's scrawl along the back: "Will you marry me?"

The last item on the keychain was a ring.

It took me what felt like a very long time to realize that this was the proposal I was waiting for. He wasn't on one knee, but he had given me the ring and asked the question. By the time I put these pieces together, Adam was in the doorway with arms full of groceries, still laughing at me. I saw his smile beneath his bright blue eyes. I saw him standing in the entryway of our home, the house we'd bought together. I saw him surrounded by the tools of our lives – food to cook for one another, coats hanging on the coat rack to keep us warm, the door to the bedroom we share, our laundry strewn across the floor and hang-drying behind him. I saw the life we had built already around us and the decades of living we had left to do all wrapped up in this keyring, this key, and this diamond ring. There was no question, of course. I had already committed my life and heart to this man, and I was glad to make that commitment public.

Ironically, the first thing I said to him was "No!" Of course, he knew this was not a denial of his proposal, but a recognition that he surprised me as much as he intended. I quickly corrected myself with a series of yeses, and we spent the rest of the evening eating those burgers and calling our family across the country. Ten months after that night we got married. We enjoyed seventeen giggly months as newlyweds, and then we welcomed our daughter.

In my previous relationships, even when I thought so confidently that I'd marry my partner, I always put years between our present and future. I wanted to finish college before deciding anything, to get my master's degree before deciding anything, to see what jobs were out there before deciding anything. If you'd asked me if I wanted to marry that boyfriend, whichever one, I'd have said yes. Because I *thought*.

But everything is different when you *know*.

Everything I've always questioned turned out to be my answer. My engagement and marriage were born from an insanely emotional period in my life. I know I would have been able to get through my grief single, but grieving alongside Adam gave me a lifeboat. No one should grieve alone, not long term. We need love from friends and family to remind us that there is light in our lives, too. And that willingness to reach out—combined with a lot of instinctual attraction—led to an engagement that even Nicholas Sparks hadn't thought of yet.

I've tried to articulate how I knew. I've tried to put all of those feelings and instincts into a formula. I just can't. My husband, from the moment we met, knew me better than I knew myself. Our first date felt like forever. From our first kiss, I couldn't imagine my life without him, and he has consistently delivered to me whatever I need, even if I get caught up in what I'm supposed to want, like with our engagement.

I still cringe a little at love stories. My tolerance for cheesiness is low, and that won't change. But I look at those "unreasonable plots" a lot differently now. It's possible that a therapist might fall in love with her patient when they go through a difficult process together. It's not exactly ethical, but there are ways to make the relationship okay.

And who's to say a couple might not change their mind after divorce when they watch their daughter find love? Forever is a long time to be together, and it takes a hell of a lot of work. A marriage is much different than a wedding. Sometimes what we call "falling out of love" is just forgetting how to do that work. There's hope they could find forever again, especially if the person they brought into this world shows them how.

I'll admit defeat, okay? I was wrong.

As soon as I lived my own love story, I recognized the truth, even if I didn't admit it right away. And three years after that first date, I used that key to lock the door before going to my wedding. I giggled the whole way down the aisle.

But the engagement is just the beginning. We've only been married for about four years, now. We still have a lot ahead of us—the rest of our lives! So, I maintain what I've said all along: the love story you want is to brush your teeth at the same sink every day for the rest of your life. The good, the bad, the ugly, it's all a part of the shared weight we carry every day.

My heart still hurts when I think about Joe. He was so young, and he hurt more than I ever realized. There were times in my life when I hurt that much, too, and Joe was one who helped me through them. I've healed quite a bit and learned how to shoulder the weight of my grief, though a part of me will always think about the what-ifs. But even when he left me, Joe found a way to make sure I was always loved. Appreciated. Happy. And it turns out that Joe, ever the hopeless romantic, also found a way to make me believe in the magic of love stories.

I just had to live one first.

Discussion Questions

1. *More Than This*: Did Terry butt in to a private disagreement at the Christmas party, or did he stand up for Steph?

2. *Someday*: What obvious and subtle challenges will Diana face in her marriage by being married to a military person?

3. *Just My Bill:* Paul asked Bill to move into a new apartment with him after two weeks. Do you think that is more risky or brave?

4. *Chatroom Love*: Besides popularity, how has online dating changed since ten years ago?

5. *Extraordinary Engagement*: Does age matter in a relationship? If it does, what is the largest gap between both parties that is still manageable?

6. *Easy*: What causes us to feel uncomfortable when things seem too easy in a relationship?

7. *Lost & Found*: This story showed that it is never too late for love. What are some of the benefits of getting together later in life?

8. *Smitten*: Mona and Ellie both enjoyed cycling. What is the importance of having similar interests and different ones in relationships?

9. *He's a Keeper*: How does having children change a relationship?

10. *A Diamond Is Forever*: Similar to the story in the introduction, Chelsea had to wait for her ring. Do you think either woman should have just proposed themselves? Why or why not?

11. *On Top of the World*: How can a preconceived notion of an event affect the person's experience?

12. *Yesterday, Today, and Forever*: How are there seasons in a marriage like there are seasons in life?

13. *All the Ordinary Moments*: There are more ordinary days than special days in a marriage. How can a person find the magic of love in the everyday?

14. *The Love Story of Margrethe*: What do you think has been the biggest change to marriage since the early 1900s?

15. *The Dance of Destiny*: How does planning a wedding prepare the couple for marriage?

16. *It's a Love Story, Afterall*: Love bloomed from tragedy in this story. How frequently does something positive come from something negative in our lives?

17. Which story did you relate to the most?

18. Was there a story where the person made a choice that would have been the opposite of what you would choose?

Meet the Authors

Stephania Thompson,
More Than This

A former CPA in the corporate world, Stephania Thompson is a published poet and multi-genre author residing outside Washington D.C. She and her husband are living the dream in their modern-day money pit with four children, a spoiled aussiedoodle, and one very moody bearded dragon.

When not writing, working, or driving carpool, she can be found running local trails or escaping in a book at her favorite café, iced latte in hand. She's a sucker for quirky romance, flawed characters, and quiet authenticity, both on and off the page.

Diana Dubs, *Someday*

D.C. Dubs always wished she could be a princess, but when that didn't work out, she became an English teacher instead. Over the past seven years, she's shared her love of reading and writing with her seventh and eighth grade students. Outside of teaching, she scribbles short stories and novels and loves to explore wherever army life takes her and her fiancé.

Paul Iasevoli, *Just My Bill*

Paul is a native New Yorker who's put down roots in Florida where he sifts words from beach sand and conjures characters out of conch shells. Before settling on the Suncoast, he earned Master's degrees in literature and language from universities in the Midwest, Canada, and Spain. Now he writes stories and poems, tucks them into empty wine bottles, and tosses them into the Gulf of Mexico. Some of them have resurfaced in literary journals such as *Deep South Magazine*, *City.River.Tree.*, *High Shelf Press*, and *Cathexis*.

Marie Montgomery, *Chatroom Love*

Marie is a 20-year public relations industry veteran now working to bring love stories to life on the written page.

When she is not working as a freelance PR professional and writer, being a mom, or trying to find some way of balancing being involved in all four of her children's lives, Marie loves indulging a great romance novel or spending whatever time she alone can manage with her husband of 17 years, who is also affectionally known as "Mr. Man."

Marie lives in Florida but is a lifelong transplant from the great state of Pennsylvania.

E.M. Hector, *Extraordinary Engagement*

Eileen is a versatile writer. She has written in many genres to include but not limited to poetry, fiction, non-fiction, memoir, and a fair amount of business writing. She often writes rhyming poetry suitable for her granddaughters, and perhaps a board book or two. Her random ramblings give her family, friends, and fan base something to either laugh out loud about or cry about. Sometimes they are even left scratching their heads.

In her spare time, should she find any, she tends to her granddaughters, a flock of birds, grows and shows orchids, and volunteers for various orchid related organizations. Other than that - she hasn't quite figured out what she wants to be when she grows up.

Dan Carroll, *Easy*

Dan Carroll grew up enjoying the woods, water, and nature of Southwest Florida. He was a single dad to his boys Danny and Baley, and he coached every sport they played. Dan believes in teaching the next generation the values of hard work, self-reliance, and the importance of the natural world. In 2016 he married Jennifer a professional artist, crafter, and content writer. Dan has worked in the pest control field since 1981 and in 2019 started a freelance writing business. He is also on the Loud.us writing team. Today Dan and Jennifer live in Port Charlotte, Fl, with their two dogs.

M.R. Shorey, *Lost & Found*

Marty Gomersall, under the name of M.R. Shorey, writes in multiple genres—all based on life experiences. "Everything, everyone has a story. Tell it!" Her short story, "The Cat Burglar," appears in the anthology, *How I Met My Other: Furry*

Friends, True Tails. Her life is beyond busy with writing and moving into a new house with her "Other" in the mountains in the high desert of New Mexico.

Mona Posinoff, *Smitten*

A true romantic, Mona jumped at the chance to share her story of finding never ending love with her forever partner, Ellie. Together they fostered and adopted Bailey Mama dog who had 10 puppies in their care and is featured in *How I Met My Other, Furry Friends, True Tails.*

Mona enjoys writing when she finally sits down and stops doing the many other activities she is involved in such as: sewing/quilting, pottery, gardening, bicycling, hiking, running, cooking, paddle boarding, baking, chanting (SGI-USA Buddhist practice), podcasting, and archery. She is slowly working on her memoir. As an avid reader, she has found truth and growth in other people's stories of success despite early years of hardship.

Mona is forever indebted to Eloise Rae Gilbert, her life partner, for always believing in her.

Check out her Podcast: Stories from A-Z with Mona P or, A-Z with Mona P on all podcasting platforms. If you would like to share your story, feel free to contact her through her FB page.

Rita Angelini, *He's a Keeper*

Rita Angelini grew up in Chicago and recently moved to Fort Myers, Florida. A retired Certified Public Accountant, she is pursuing her passion for writing. She is the mother of Marina, a typically developing daughter, and KiKi, who drafted Rita into the world of special needs. People are thrust into the realm of disability, a world unto itself, with no manual. Rita became an expert in her daughter. KiKi's disability pushed her to find alternative options in order for KiKi to reach her potential. KiKi's life compelled Rita to share their story and unfortunately, KiKi's premature death gave Rita the opportunity to write about it.

She is a member of Off Campus Writers' Workshop in Illinois and has been the Treasurer for the last seven years. She is also a member of Florida Writers Association, Gulf Coast Writers Association, and the National Association of Memoir Writers.

She published a short story, *Screensaver*, in *Turning Points*, an anthology. She plans to publish her memoir about life with her daughter, KiKi, who teaches her family about compassion, faith, and unconditional love without speaking a word. When Rita is not writing, she is volunteering with the disabled, boating on the Gulf, or traveling the country in her RV.

Chelsea Fuchs, *A Diamond Is Forever*

Chelsea Fuchs is an engineer by day and an author by night. Her background in STEM combined with her cowgirl heart heavily influences her characters and stories. Being addicted to sweet romances and management books herself, Chelsea writes strong female leads in nontraditional roles. When she's not at work, she's busy keeping her littles from taking over the world, writing women's fiction, and managing the farm her and her husband just purchased. Chelsea lives in New Mexico with her (almost) high school sweetheart, their son and daughter, and a collection of animals that would give Noah a run for his money..

Renee Adamowicz-Schwartz, *On Top of the World*

Renee has always loved writing her thoughts, but she never enjoyed the rules and correctness of it all. She has been told she writes like she speaks and speaks what she thinks. She hopes to share this great adventure with love and passion. She and her husband Chuck enjoy a great life on a cozy South Carolina Island walking the beach, living out adventures, and live each day with passion, peace, gratefulness, and love.

Sharon Rhyce, *Yesterday, Today, and Forever*

Formerly an elementary teacher, now retired, Sharon Rhyce lives On the West Coast of Florida. She enjoys dabbling in writing, crafting, exploring family history, traveling as well as offering private tutoring for elementary students. She's blessed with a wonderful husband, three dear adult children and a lovely daughter-in-love. She's a proud dog mom of Chico, a spoiled Chiweenie. The cherry on top is her precocious granddaughter, Audrey, who stole her heart from day one.

Miranda L. Scotti, *All the Ordinary Moments*

Miranda L. Scotti is a lifelong author and daydreamer who found her voice writing contemporary romance after experiencing her own happily ever after. She works in a library to maximize her time spent drinking coffee while surrounded by shelves of books. Miranda lives in with her incredible family and lazy tabby cat. A lifelong Floridian, she has never found a spot in the state she loves more than under the giant Southern Oak tree where she and her husband fell in love.

Madonna Dries Christensen, *The Love Story of Margrethe*

Madonna Dries Christensen cut her writer's teeth on family history. Her immigrant ancestors were German, French-Canadian, and Irish. Among treasured memorabilia is a stone from the foundation of her great-grandfather's Wisconsin barn, a plank from her grandfather's Iowa barn with her father's initials carved in it, and her mother's wedding band. She has a Christensen family history back to the 1700s. It's mostly names and dates, with Danish narrative. There's also a trunk, hand-crafted in Denmark in 1890, like the one in Margrethe's Love Story.

Margrethe was Madonna's husband's aunt and Kristian (Chris) was his father. Margrethe's and

Marinus's family were known as "the California cousins." Born on an Iowa farm in 1935, Madonna lives with her husband in Sarasota, Florida.

Jasmine Tritten, *Dance of Destiny*

Jasmine Tritten is an award-winning author and artist born in Denmark. In 1964 she immigrated to the U.S.A. She has been journaling since childhood. The last six years she has written numerous short stories published in various anthologies. In 2015 she published her memoir *The Journey of an Adventuresome Dane*. She wrote and illustrated a children's story *Kato's*

Grand Adventure, published in 2018. During the pandemic in 2020, Jasmine wrote, illustrated, and published a travel memoir *On the Nile with a Dancing Dane.* She resides in enchanting Corrales, New Mexico with her husband and four cats.

Jenna Wilson, *It's a Love Story, Afterall*

Jenna Wilson currently resides in Central Illinois with her family. She works as a high school English teacher and runs a home bakery. Her passion is writing contemporary fiction and free verse poetry, but the memoir published here is a story kept close to her heart.

Meet the Editor

Arielle Haughee

Arielle Haughee (Hoy) is a six-time RPLA-winning author, editor, speaker, and publisher. She writes a mix of children's picture books and adult nonfiction. After launching Orange Blossom Publishing in 2017, she discovered her love of being "behind the scenes" with books and expanded into a small press. She lives in Central Florida and loves dogs, babies, purple, and bacon.

More in This Series

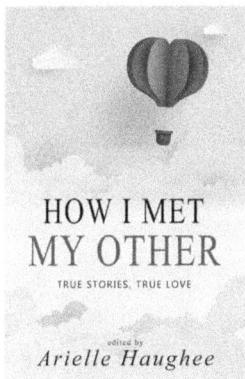

How I Met My Other, Volume 1: True Stories, True Love

Learn about all the twists, turns, and fun of falling in love with this unforgettable true story anthology.

People find the warmth of love in Antarctica. An obsession with blondes lands the big one. Squashing a guitar case leads to a blanket fort date. A soldier works to snag a sassy WWII nurse. A revenge date gets serious. Spaghetti reels someone in and they never go home again. And much, much more!

Love can come at the most surprising times and in the most unexpected places. In this short story collection, fifteen authors share their incredible, heart-warming, and often hilarious true tales of how they met their other.

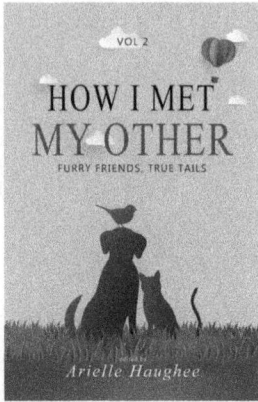

How I Met My Other, Volume 2: Furry Friends, True Tails

Nothing is like the warmth, fun, and unconditional love of a pet. In this collection of twenty true stories, pet owners share the life-changing moments they met that special cat, dog, and even llama. Laugh at the goofballs that leap to amazing heights, lead parades, try to take over the house, and find creative ways to show their dissatisfaction. Feel the love of the sweethearts who help their owners make it through illness and emotional challenges. Experience the strength and total devotion of these special animals. Join us in celebrating one of life's greatest gifts: the never-ending love of a pet.

Did you enjoy this book?

Please consider leaving a review on Amazon or Good Reads. It helps our small press sell more books!

[QR codes for Amazon and GoodReads, links for ebook]

www.ingramcontent.com/pod-product-compliance
Lightning Source LLC
Chambersburg PA
CBHW032050020426
42335CB00011B/267